DATE DUE

PRESIDENTS
By Accident

Also by Edmund Lindop

**THE BILL OF RIGHTS
AND LANDMARK CASES**

PRESIDENTS
By Accident
EDMUND LINDOP

FRANKLIN WATTS
NEW YORK/LONDON/TORONTO/SYDNEY/1991

Photographs copyright ©: Rothco Cartoons: p. 1; Historical Pictures
Service: pp. 2, 3 bottom, 4, 6, 7, 15; The Bettmann Archive: pp. 3 top,
9; Culver Pictures, Inc.: pp. 3, 8, 10; Brown Brothers: pp. 11, 12;
UPI/Bettmann Newsphotos: pp. 13, 14, 16.

Library of Congress Cataloging-in-Publication Data

Lindop, Edmund.
Presidents by accident / by Edmund Lindop.
p.   cm.
Includes bibliographical references and index.
Summary: Discusses the nine vice-presidents of the United States
who became president when the office fell suddenly vacant because of
death or resignation.
ISBN 0-531-11059-1
1. Vice-Presidents—United States—Biography—Juvenile literature.
2. Presidents—United States—Biography—Juvenile literature.
3. Presidents—United States—Succession—Juvenile literature.
[1. Vice-Presidents. 2. Presidents. 3. Presidents—Succession.]
I. Title.
E176.49.L56 1991
973'.0992—dc20
[B]   91-17056
CIP
AC

CONTENTS

It is a mighty leap from the Vice Presidency to the Presidency when one is forced to make it without warning. Under the present system a Vice President cannot equip himself to become President merely by virtue of being second in rank.
—Harry S Truman

Prologue

When the Republican convention assembled at New Orleans in August 1988, it was a foregone conclusion that Vice President George Bush would be its presidential candidate. But most political observers were stunned when Bush asked the convention to name as his vice presidential running mate the junior senator from Indiana, J. Danforth (Dan) Quayle. The handsome forty-one-year-old Quayle was little known outside Washington, D.C., and his home state.

Media reporters scrambled to find out more about Dan Quayle, and their search produced several troublesome questions. Had Quayle joined the National Guard to escape fighting in the Vietnam War? Had members of his wealthy, prominent family used their influence to secure his enlistment in the Guard? Did his mediocre college record indicate he wasn't very bright? Had his family pulled any strings to help him get into law school? Why didn't his colleagues in Congress regard him as one of their leaders and praise his selection as a vice presidential nominee?

During the election campaign, more doubts were raised about Quayle's qualifications. His remarks were laced with garbled sentences, and some statements sounded inane. In his one debate with the Democratic vice presidential candidate, Senator Lloyd Bentsen of Texas, Quayle's performance was hesitant, confused, and generally weak. As the campaign progressed, Quayle was portrayed by the media as an inept puppet whose every public appearance was carefully controlled and orchestrated by shrewd professional image-makers.

A large segment of the American public became concerned about Quayle's questionable background, his maturity and judgment, and even his basic intelligence. People were less worried about his ability to perform the virtually powerless duties of the vice presidency than they were about what would happen if he were suddenly elevated to the presidency.

These doubts about whether Quayle could be a competent president actually increased after the 1988 election. Gallup polls showed the percentage of Americans who believed Quayle was qualified to become president dropped from 46 percent in October 1988 to 34 percent in May 1989 to 31 percent in March 1990. Those Americans who felt Quayle was unqualified to become president rose from 42 percent in the fall of 1988 to 52 percent in the spring of 1990. When the United States became involved in the Persian Gulf War in January 1991, pollsters for *Time* magazine asked the public, "If something happened to President Bush, are you confident that Vice President Quayle could lead the nation in the war with Iraq?" More than half of those who replied— 55 percent—said no, while only 28 percent said yes.

The question of a vice president's qualifications

10

to become the chief executive cannot be dismissed lightly. Three of the ten presidents between 1945 and 1990 had been vice presidents who assumed the highest office in the land because of the death or resignation of the president under whom they had served. Of the forty men who have been president of the United States, nine of them (nearly one-fourth) reached that position because they had been vice presidents called upon to complete the term of a president.

This book discusses each of these nine "accidental" presidents. It tells about their home backgrounds, their personalities and beliefs, their political experiences before they reached the White House, and, most important, their accomplishments and shortcomings as president.

Harry Truman, the vice president who succeeded to the presidency upon the death of Franklin D. Roosevelt, recalled what it was like to have the reins of government suddenly thrust into his hands. "Within the first few months," he said, "I discovered that being a President is like riding a tiger. A man has to keep on riding or be swallowed." [1]

The chief purpose of this book is to reveal how well each of the nine "presidents by accident" rode that tiger.

Chapter 1
A Heartbeat Away

In the first few years after the United States became an independent country, there were no separate elections for president and vice president. The Constitution provided that every member of the Electoral College would have two votes. After these official electors cast their ballots, the candidate who received the most votes would be president and the candidate with the next largest number of votes would be vice president. The Founding Fathers believed this procedure would guarantee that the best-qualified candidate would become the nation's chief executive and the second-best-qualified candidate would assume the second-highest position in the government.

This system worked well in the first two presidential elections. In both, George Washington was the electors' unanimous choice for president and John Adams, who had fewer electoral votes than Washington, became vice president. But with the development of two different political parties the system began to break down. In the 1796 election, Federal-

ist John Adams was elected president, but the runner-up who became vice president was Thomas Jefferson, the presidential candidate of the Democratic-
Republican party. The system was fatally flawed by
the outcome of the 1800 election, in which every
Democratic-Republican elector loyally cast one vote
for Jefferson, the party's presidential candidate, and
the other vote for the party's vice presidential nominee, Aaron Burr. As a result, Jefferson and Burr
were tied in the electoral vote and the election was
thrown into the House of Representatives, which elects
the president if no candidate has more than half of
the electoral vote. The House voted to make Jefferson president and Burr vice president.

The procedure for electing the president and vice
president was radically changed by the Twelfth
Amendment, ratified in 1804. This constitutional
amendment required electors to indicate which of
their two votes was for a presidential candidate and
which was for a vice presidential candidate. Ever since
1804, there have been separate elections for president and vice president.

While the Twelfth Amendment solved one electoral problem, it created another. Vice presidential
candidates no longer were necessarily selected on the
basis of being the most capable person available for
inheriting the presidency. Instead, the political parties tended to choose a vice presidential nominee who
they felt was the best candidate to help elect the
president.

The politicians' desire to win elections led to
"balancing the ticket," a practice whereby a vice
presidential candidate was selected because that person could attract voter support in areas where the
presidential candidate was thought to be weak. Some
vice presidential candidates were chosen because they
came from a geographic region different from that

14

of the presidential nominee. Or they represented a different faction of their political party. Or they strongly appealed to certain groups of voters, such as farmers or minorities, who might have been less enthusiastic about the candidate at the top of the ticket. At times other factors, such as religion, physical appearance, speaking ability, and temperament, were considered when the yardstick of balancing the ticket was applied to possible vice presidential candidates. In 1984, when Democratic Congresswoman Geraldine Ferraro was the first woman nominated for the vice presidency by either major political party, gender became another factor in balancing the ticket.

In the nineteenth century and the first part of the twentieth century, some presidents and their vice presidents sharply disagreed on important government policies. Theodore Roosevelt recognized the danger in these two officials having widely different opinions when he wrote, "It is an unhealthy thing to have the Vice-President and the President represented by principles so far apart that the succession of one to the place of the other means a change as radical as any party overturn."[1]

In the last half century, however, the presidential candidate usually has announced whom he preferred as a running mate, and then the party convention accepted his recommendation. This procedure has created much more harmony between the two highest officeholders in the executive department. While balancing the ticket still is practiced, the possibility of serious clashes between the president and vice president has been greatly reduced.

The only constitutional duties assigned to the vice president are to preside over the Senate and, in the event of a tie vote in that chamber, to cast the tie-breaking vote. (In practice, the vice president seldom attends Senate sessions; one of the senators is as-

signed to take his place at the rostrum.) The first
Congress, aware that the vice president had little to
do, debated whether to pay that officeholder any salary and finally settled on a measly $5,000 a year as
adequate pay.

Vice President John Adams agreed that his position was indeed powerless and declared that it was
"the most insignificant office that ever the invention
of man contrived."[2] Many of the persons who later
held the same office shared Adams's low opinion of
it. A frustrated Theodore Roosevelt felt he had moved
from the limelight into the shadows when he had
been pressured to give up the governorship of New
York for the vice presidency. Thomas R. Marshall,
Woodrow Wilson's vice president, used to tell the story
of two brothers: one went to sea, the other was elected
vice president, and nothing was ever heard of either
again.[3] John Nance Garner, who served as vice president during the first two terms of Franklin D. Roosevelt's administration, compared his office unfavor-
ably to "a pitcher of warm spit."[4]

Some ambitious politicians avoided the vice
presidency as if it were a plague. In 1844 New York
Senator Silas Wright was formally chosen by the
Democratic convention as its vice presidential candidate but he refused the nomination. The same thing
occurred in 1924, when former Governor Frank
Lowden of Illinois turned down the Republican
nomination for the vice presidency. And, in 1832,
Vice President John C. Calhoun paid his office the
supreme indignity: he resigned to seek a seat in the
Senate, where he felt his influence would be much
greater.

Others besides politicians have held the vice
presidency in low regard. Some historians have rec-
ommended that the office be abolished, saying that
if a president died or became disabled, a temporary

16

president (perhaps the secretary of state) should head the government until a special election could be held.[5] Pollsters have found that in presidential elections only a small percentage of the electorate say that their opinions of vice presidential candidates strongly influence the way that they vote.[6] Even musical composers have poked fun at the vice presidency. In *Of Thee I Sing*, a 1931 Pulitzer Prize–winning musical satire, Vice President Alexander Throttlebottom was a forlorn character whose name no one remembered and who dared not mention the position he held lest his mother find out about it and be humiliated. Poor Throttlebottom had so little access to the president that he had to join a guided tour to get into the White House.

Theodore Roosevelt asserted that the vice presidency "is not a stepping stone to anything except oblivion."[7] While this did not prove to be true in his case because he ascended to the presidency upon the death of William McKinley in 1901, only four times in American history has a president, on retiring from office, handed the keys to the White House to his vice president. John Adams and Thomas Jefferson both became president immediately after their vice presidential terms ended. In 1836 Vice President Martin Van Buren was elected president to replace retiring Andrew Jackson. More than a century and a half passed before this event was repeated again, when George Bush succeeded Ronald Reagan in the Oval Office.

Little was done before 1921 to heighten the status of the vice presidency. In that year, Warren G. Harding became the first president to make his vice president, Calvin Coolidge, a regular (though unofficial) member of his cabinet. When Coolidge became president he expected Vice President Charles G. Dawes to follow this precedent, but Dawes declared that under no circumstances would he attend cabinet meetings. Dawes felt it was a poor idea to let a vice president have a voice in policy decisions because, in case of a strong difference of opinion, the president could fire a cabinet member but couldn't get rid of a vice president until the end of his term. Franklin D. Roosevelt revived vice presidential attendance at cabinet meetings, and since his administration this has been an established practice.

During the past fifty years, more duties and responsibilities have been assigned to vice presidents. Often they serve as stand-ins for the president at official functions, such as inaugurations, weddings, and funerals. In 1949 President Harry Truman persuaded Congress to pass a law making the vice president a member of the National Security Council. This important White House council includes high officials in the executive department who help the president make crucial decisions on foreign and defense matters.

President Jimmy Carter handed Vice President Walter F. Mondale more responsibilities in the day-to-day process of running the government than any previous vice president ever had. But Mondale's most important function was to advise the president on most major issues that reached the White House. Mondale declared that the vice president "has a right to be heard" by the president—but "not obeyed."[8]

When George Bush became Ronald Reagan's vice president, he headed special task forces to fight terrorism and the international drug trade. After the attempt to assassinate President Reagan in March 1981, Bush presided over cabinet meetings and conferred with government leaders while the president recuperated. Another time, Bush served for a short while as "acting president," in accordance with a provision of the Twenty-fifth Amendment that deals with presidential disability. In July 1985, just before President Reagan underwent surgery for colon cancer, he signed a temporary transfer of presidential power to Bush, which went into effect during the brief period while Reagan was under anesthesia. (Provisions of the Twenty-fifth Amendment pertaining to presidential succession are discussed in Chapter 10.)

After Bush became president, among the duties he delegated to Vice President Dan Quayle was the task of heading the National Space Council. This is an intergovernmental panel designed to coordinate the nation's space activities.

Although it has been given additional responsibilities and duties in recent years, the vice presidency still is less important in the operation of the government's executive branch than several other offices, including those held by department heads who serve on the cabinet and by other key advisers to the president. The one and only aspect of the vice presidency that is of enormous significance is that the person who holds it is just a heartbeat away from the presidency. Vice President John Adams recognized this paradox when he said, "In this, I am nothing. But I could be everything."[9]

Chapter 2
John Tyler: States' Rights President

John Tyler, Sr., father of the tenth president, belonged to the planter aristocracy and played an active role in the political affairs of Virginia. Like his friend and college roommate, Thomas Jefferson, he believed strongly in the rights of states. Tyler and Jefferson both feared that a powerful national government would ride roughshod over state governments and leave them weak and unable to function effectively.

After the Constitution was written, lawyer Tyler was a member of Virginia's convention summoned to consider its ratification. Since he favored continuation of the weak Articles of Confederation government with its loose union of sovereign states, Tyler vigorously attacked the Constitution. "Little did I think," he thundered, "that matters would come to this when we separated from the mother country."[1]

In spite of the opposition of Tyler and other patriots like Patrick Henry and Richard Henry Lee, the Virginia convention ratified the Constitution by the

20

narrow vote of eighty-nine votes for it and seventy-nine against. This bitterly disappointed Tyler, but his interest in politics continued. He later served in two important government positions—as governor of Virginia, and judge of the United States Circuit Court.

Judge Tyler's eight children grew up on a large plantation in Charles City County, not far from Richmond, Virginia. John, the second-oldest son, who was born in 1790, continued in his father's political footsteps. Young John was eager to learn, and in 1802, at the age of twelve, he entered the grammar school division of William and Mary College in Williamsburg, Virginia. Later he took college courses at the same school. He was especially interested in ancient history, political science, Latin, Shakespeare, and poetry. And a love of music led him to become an accomplished violinist.

After his graduation from William and Mary, Tyler started studying law with his father. (At that time it was common for would-be lawyers to receive their legal training from experienced attorneys.) Within two years he was admitted to the bar and began practicing law. Legal and social success came readily to him. He had a pleasant voice, courtly manners, and a genial wit that often brought smiles to a solemn courtroom and made him the center of social functions. Tyler's appearance also commanded attention: he was six feet tall, slender, with blue eyes, light brown hair, and a thin Roman nose.

Tyler's personal popularity helped him easily win election to the Virginia House of Delegates in 1811 when he was only twenty-one years old. He was reelected to the Virginia legislature every year for five years. Then, in 1816, he was elected to fill a vacancy in the United States House of Representatives.

Meanwhile, in 1813, Tyler married Letitia Christian, the daughter of another Virginia planter.

They eventually had five sons and three daughters. Supporting such a large family on a meager government salary and the small profits from the sale of their farm crops was difficult, but Letitia and John saved every penny they could and managed to send their sons to William and Mary College.

While Tyler was serving his second term as a congressman, a question that came before the House was whether slavery should be permitted in the new territory acquired as a result of the Louisiana Purchase. A compromise was reached whereby Missouri would be admitted to the Union as a slave state and Maine (not part of the Louisiana Purchase) as a free state, but slavery would be prohibited in the rest of the Louisiana Territory north of 36°30′ latitude. Though he had slaves himself, Tyler believed that slavery was a degrading institution that would gradually wither away. But he felt that Congress had no legitimate power to tell the people of a territory or state whether they could or could not keep slaves. So Tyler voted against the so-called Missouri Compromise and was unhappy when the measure passed. Disappointed that he had lost this fight and temporarily in ill health, Tyler declined to run for reelection in 1820.

His political career, however, was far from ended. Two years later he again became a member of the Virginia House of Delegates, and in 1825, like his father before him, he was elected governor of Virginia. While Tyler headed the state government, he worked to develop a system of roads and canals that helped link coastal Virginia with the less settled western part of the state. Soon, however, he tired of being governor and wanted to return to Congress, where the nation's laws are made. He was elected to the Senate in 1827 and served there until 1836.

Tyler's early political allegiance was to the Jeffersonian Democratic-Republican party, which ardently championed states' rights. But the party of Thomas Jefferson, which shortened its name to "Democratic," began to change when it fell under the control of war hero Andrew Jackson in the late 1820s and 1830s. Although Tyler voted for Jackson for president in both 1828 and 1832, he gradually became disillusioned with aspects of "King Andrew's" rule. Jackson, Tyler believed, had become a dictator whose nationalistic policies were undermining the powers of the states. The Virginia aristocrat also disapproved of Jackson's obvious attempt to woo the common people.

An issue that widened the schism between Senator Tyler and President Jackson stemmed from South Carolina's determination to nullify (refuse to enforce) an 1832 law calling for high tariffs (tariffs are taxes on imports). When South Carolina declared that these tariffs would not be collected at its ports, the president asked Congress for the authority to use military force to make that state conform to the law. Tyler did not approve of nullification, but he was even more strongly opposed to the federal government's use of force against South Carolina.

When the so-called Force Bill came to a Senate vote, many southern legislators agreed with Tyler's position. But, hoping for some compromise on the tariff issue, they stayed away from the Senate chamber rather than have their votes recorded on this controversial bill. Senator Tyler was the only one of the bill's opponents who had the courage to vote his convictions.

Like Jackson, Tyler felt that the Bank of the United States, or national bank, was unconstitutional. However, the Virginia senator argued that the president had abused his powers when he removed the government deposits in the national bank and placed them in various state banks. In 1834 an angry Senate censured (officially criticized) Jackson for removing the public funds, but the following year the president's supporters resolved to have the censure stricken from the Senate journal. The Virginia legislature instructed Tyler to vote for removal of the censure, but he refused to do so. Rather than vote for something that his conscience told him was wrong, Tyler resigned his Senate seat.

Tyler's break with President Jackson and the Democratic party now was complete. He joined the young Whig party, which consisted almost entirely of people who for one reason or another disliked Jackson. The largest and most popular faction of the Whig party was headed by senators Henry Clay and Daniel Webster. Clay put forth what was known as the American System, an ambitious plan that called for high protective tariffs to please the northern manufacturers, federally financed roads and canals to please western and southern farmers, and a new national bank to replace the one that President Jackson had destroyed. Although Tyler opposed all of these proposals, he became a Whig because this was the only political party in which he and other states' rights southerners could vent their anger against Jackson and his Democratic cronies.

In the 1836 election the Whig party was not yet sufficiently organized to hold a national convention and select a presidential candidate who could appeal to all sections of the country. Instead, it ran Senator Daniel Webster of New Hampshire in Massachusetts, Senator Hugh White of Tennessee in the South, and General William Henry Harrison of Ohio in the rest of the nation. The Whigs named Francis Granger of New York as Harrison's and Webster's running mate and Tyler to run for vice president with White. The Whig leaders realized that none of their three presidential candidates could outpoll Democrat Martin Van Buren, Jackson's handpicked nominee to succeed himself in the White House. But they hoped the combined Whig vote would deny Van Buren a majority and force the election into the House of Representatives.

Van Buren won the presidency, but the Whigs were heartened because their three candidates together amassed over 49 percent of the popular vote. General Harrison led the other Whig contenders, winning 550,816 votes to Van Buren's 764,176.

Shortly after Van Buren moved into the White House, a financial panic occurred. The country sank into a deep depression that was to last for several years. Many voters blamed the party in power for these hard times. Then too, Van Buren lacked Jackson's rough-hewn charisma and dominant personality that had won the allegiance of many farmers and city workers. "Old Hickory" had become the champion of democracy and the symbol of the common man (even though he was a prosperous planter). But Jackson was unable to transfer this image to Van Buren, a short, plump man who seemed rather pompous and more interested in social activities at the White House than in the needs of the ordinary people.

Aware of Van Buren's weaknesses, the Whigs looked to the 1840 election as an excellent opportunity to capture the White House. Henry Clay, who had run unsuccessfully for president in 1824 and 1832, felt certain that the party would name him its standard-bearer; he was a towering force in the Senate and the nation's most prominent Whig. But other Whig chieftains were not confident that a two-time loser could topple Van Buren. They wanted to play it safe—nominate a popular, rugged war hero who, like Jackson, would stir the electorate's patriotism.

General Harrison had the necessary military credentials: in 1811 he had put down an Indian uprising at Tippecanoe, in what is now Indiana, and during the War of 1812 he had served as one of the country's few successful generals. Moreover, in 1836 he had run a strong race against Van Buren.

So the Whig convention chose "Old Tip," rather than Clay, to oppose the Democratic protégé of "Old Hickory." And to draw southern votes to the ticket it named Tyler as his running mate.

Clay was furious when he learned that the Whigs had bypassed him. "It is a diabolical intrigue, I know now, which has betrayed me," he sputtered. "I am the most unfortunate man in the history of parties: always run by my friends when sure to be defeated, and now betrayed for a nomination when I, or any one, would be sure of election."[2]

Whig leaders softened the blow to Clay's pride by assuring him that he would wield the real power behind the throne. Harrison had already declared that, if elected, he would leave policy-making to Congress, where Clay had enormous influence. And the sixty-eight-year-old general pledged not to seek a second term, which left the door open to a Clay candidacy in 1844.

The Whig convention did not risk destruction of its fragile unity by writing a party platform, since it would have offended either Clay's nationalists or Tyler's states' righters. The absence of a platform, Clay's supporters reasoned, would make it easier for Clay to gain acceptance of his policies from a submissive president like Harrison. But apparently no one at the convention had bothered to consider what would happen if the elderly Harrison died in office and was succeeded by a vice president who loathed most of Clay's important goals!

The 1840 presidential election provided one of

the most exciting and colorful campaigns in our political history. Both sides had huge rallies, rousing speeches, and lengthy parades, but the Whigs happened upon a gimmick that gave them an unexpected giant boost. A Baltimore political correspondent, poking fun at Harrison, wrote: "Give him a barrel of hard cider and a pension of two thousand a year and, my word for it, he will sit the remainder of his days in a log cabin. . . ."

The Whigs cleverly turned this intended slur into a winning slogan. Even though Harrison had come from a prosperous plantation family, his supporters began picturing him as the log-cabin and hard-cider candidate, a plain, down-to-earth man who appreciated the problems of the common people because he was one of them. At the same time they portrayed Van Buren as a somewhat effeminate president who rode in a gilded coach, ate with gold spoons and forks, wore diamond rings and lace shirts, and sprayed himself with the same expensive cologne that Queen Victoria used.

The log cabin symbol swept across the country. Nearly every city, town, and hamlet had at least one of these "humble Harrison houses" erected in a conspicuous place. In torchlight parades, sweating Whigs dragged floats bearing miniature log cabins, decked themselves in coonskin caps, and ladled out hard cider to thirsty voters. There were thousands of log cabin leaflets, log cabin songbooks, Tippecanoe badges, and Tippecanoe handkerchiefs. And one of the many popular ditties highlighted the slogan that would be remembered for generations to come:

What has caused this great commotion, motion,
Our country through?
It is the ball a-rolling on,
For Tippecanoe and Tyler too, Tippecanoe and Tyler too.

27

And with them we'll beat the little Van, Van, Van;
Van is a used-up man,
And with them we'll beat the little Van!

The ticket of "Tippecanoe and Tyler too" won at the polls, carrying nineteen states to Van Buren's seven. About 80 percent of the nation's eligible voters cast their ballots, establishing a record turnout for a presidential election.

On a frigid, windswept fourth of March, 1841, "Old Tip" took the presidential oath. For nearly two hours he stood on the east portico of the Capitol, bareheaded and without an overcoat, reading his rambling inaugural address, the longest on record. Again he pledged not to run for a second term or try to dictate to Congress, and he promised to use his veto sparingly.

The new president caught cold at the ceremonies and later contracted pneumonia. Doctors prescribed all the treatments used at that time—including suction cups applied to his right side and doses of snakewood root, castor oil, crude petroleum, brandy, and opium—but to no avail. Harrison died on April 4, exactly one month after his inauguration.

Tyler, who felt that his vice presidential duties were not important enough to keep him in Washington, D.C., much of the time, was at home in Virginia when a messenger on horseback brought him the startling news of Harrison's death. He hurried back to the capital, but his wife, who had been partially paralyzed by a stroke in 1839, followed her husband later.

The nation was stunned by the unprecedented death of a president in office. "It makes the Vice-President of the United States, John Tyler of Virginia, Acting President of the Union for four years less one month," wrote former President John Quincy

28

Adams in his diary. "In upwards of half a century," Adams continued, "this is the first instance of a Vice-President being called to act as President of the United States, and brings to the test that provision of the Constitution which places in the Executive chair a man never thought of for it by anybody."[3]

The provision of the Constitution to which Adams referred is indeed vague and subject to different interpretations. The Constitution says, "In case of the Removal of the President from Office, or of his Death, Resignation, or Inability to discharge the Powers and Duties of the said Office, the same shall devolve on the Vice President. . . ." An argument arose in 1841 as to whether "the same" refers to the words "Powers and Duties" or the word "Office." (This was not clarified until the 1967 adoption of the Twenty-fifth Amendment, which states that if the president dies, resigns, or is removed, "the Vice President shall become President.")

Adams and many of his political colleagues claimed that Tyler was only an "acting president," but the stubborn Virginian insisted that he *was* the new president and entitled to the salary and all the powers and privileges of that office. To emphasize this point, he had a judge administer to him the presidential oath, even though he felt this was an unnecessary gesture.

It took little time for President Tyler to make it clear that he did not intend to be a mere figurehead, a pawn in the hands of either Congress or his cabinet. At Tyler's first cabinet meeting, Secretary of State Daniel Webster explained that Harrison's practice had been to have all policy decisions determined by a majority vote, with the president's vote counting no more than that of any cabinet member. Tyler brusquely rejected this procedure, declaring, "I am the president, and I shall be held responsible for my administration. But I can never consent to being dictated as to what I shall or shall not do." Then he added bluntly, "When you think otherwise, your resignations will be accepted."[4]

Tyler also informed Henry Clay that he would not be his puppet and sign every bill that the prominent Whig leader steered through Congress. Reportedly he pointed his finger at Clay when the Kentucky senator paid him a courtesy call and said, "Go you now, then, Mr. Clay, to your end of the avenue, where stands the Capitol, and there perform your duty to the country as you shall think proper. So help me God, I shall do mine at this end of it as I shall think proper."[5]

Clay, however, was determined to promote his American System, of which a new national bank was the cornerstone. His bill for such a bank was approved by Congress and sent to the president for his signature. But Tyler vetoed the bill, asserting that the kind of national bank proposed by Clay was unconstitutional. Congress then made some minor changes in the legislation to try to placate the president. But Tyler also vetoed this second bank bill, declaring that it too was unconstitutional and failed to provide proper safeguards for the rights of the states.

Tyler's veto of the second bank bill unleashed a torrent of violent criticism from other Whigs. On September 11 about fifty enraged Whig congressmen gathered in front of the Capitol, vehemently denounced the president, and declared that he no longer belonged to their political party. Many of them called for his immediate resignation. Soon the beleaguered president was saddled with nasty nicknames—"His Accidency," "The Accident of an Accident," and "An Executive Ass." In town after town Tyler was burned in effigy, and an influenza epidemic that swept the nation was called "Tyler grippe."

Three days after Tyler became a president without a party, he also became a president without a cabinet. On that morning every member of his cabinet handed in his resignation, except Secretary of State Webster, who was in the midst of negotiating an important treaty with Great Britain and wanted to finish the task. That afternoon Webster called on the president and asked whether he too should resign.

"You must decide that for yourself," Tyler answered.

A smile creased Webster's lips and he exclaimed, "If you leave it to me, Mr. President, I will stay where I am."

The president rose from his chair, reached out his hand, and warmly said, "Give me your hand on that, and now I will say that Henry Clay is a doomed man."[6]

Clay and his Whig cohorts, however, continued their war against the president. Twice Clay proposed and Congress passed bills for higher tariffs, but Tyler vetoed these measures. Only when the government desperately needed more money did the president reluctantly agree to a raise in tariffs. In all, Tyler vetoed ten bills, the second-highest total by any president to that time. And Tyler found it virtually impossible to initiate any legislation that an antagonistic Congress would approve.

Senators and congressmen carried their vendetta against the president to the ridiculous extent that they even refused to give him the money routinely required for the upkeep of the White House. Visitors to the executive mansion during this troubled period were appalled by its shabby, run-down appearance, and some were concerned that if the president resigned he might try to slip out of Washington with valuable White House furnishings. English author Charles Dickens, who called on the president in 1841, observed that a few visitors "were closely eyeing the movables, as to make quite sure that the president (who was far from popular) had not made away with any of the furniture, or sold the fixtures for his private benefit."[7]

Apparently Tyler, the stubborn fighter, gave no serious thought to resigning the presidency, but in January 1843 he was confronted by the ultimate indignity: possible impeachment. Whig Congressman John Botts of Virginia drew up a list of charges against the president and proposed a resolution in the House of Representatives calling for a committee to investigate these charges. But even though many Whigs considered Tyler a traitor to his party, it would have been difficult to prove he had committed offenses that could be punished by removal from office. So the impeachment resolution was defeated by a vote of 83 in favor to 127 against.

Tyler's political problems were only part of the trouble he faced. In September 1842 Letitia, his frail wife of nearly thirty years, died. The president was grief-stricken and dreaded the thought of returning to the home in Virginia where they and their children had enjoyed happy times. He decided to buy another plantation in his home state and took great interest in the extensive remodeling and expansion of the main house on this property. Tyler called his new estate Sherwood Forest (the name given to the site of outlaw Robin Hood's adventures) as a whimsical reference to his outlaw status in the Whig party.

Four months after the death of his wife, Tyler began courting Julia Gardiner, the attractive, vivacious daughter of Senator David Gardiner of New York. They enjoyed each other's company, but Julia was reluctant to accept Tyler's proposal of marriage because of the difference in their ages. The president was fifty-four; she was twenty-four. Tyler's eldest daughter was five years older than his prospective bride.

One day in February 1844 the president invited Senator Gardiner and his daughter to be his guests on the naval frigate U.S.S. *Princeton* when it sailed down the Potomac River. The chief purpose of the outing would be the firing of the huge "Peacemaker," the world's largest naval gun. About 350 prominent Washington citizens, including many government officials, gathered on the ship for this gala occasion.

Twice the "Peacemaker" was fired, and each loud boom was celebrated by cheers from the assembled crowd. Then the guests went to the salon below deck for champagne toasts and a lavish buffet. It was agreed that the huge gun would be fired one more time, when the ship passed Mount Vernon, as a salute to the memory of George Washington. President Tyler and Miss Gardiner were planning to climb back to the open deck for this final firing, but they tarried below for a few minutes to hear the president's son sing a ballad.

Just as the young man was finishing his song, the "Peacemaker" was fired again. A deafening roar followed, and the *Princeton* lurched to one side. A stream of black smoke poured into the salon that a moment before had been the scene of happy festivities. The breech of the mighty "Peacemaker" had exploded, hurling huge chunks of blazing-hot iron around the deck.

Tyler and Julia hurried up the steps to the top deck. There, amid the burning debris, lay the bodies of eight men, including two members of the president's cabinet. When Julia learned that her father was among those who had been killed, she fainted. A rescue vessel was hastily summoned for the remaining people on board, and Tyler carried Julia in his arms across its gangplank.

Julia was deeply saddened by the loss of her father, but within a few weeks after the *Princeton* disaster, she agreed to marry her much older suitor. "After I lost my father I felt differently toward the President," she remarked many years later. "He seemed to fill the place and to be more agreeable in every way than any younger man ever was or could be."[8] On June 26, 1844, John Tyler became the first president to marry in office. Later, when he and Julia had five sons and two daughters, he became the president with the largest number of children—fifteen. Tyler was seventy years old when his last child was born.

There were a few accomplishments in foreign affairs to which President Tyler could point with pride. He was successful in obtaining a treaty with China to open its ports to American trade. When the native ruler of Hawaii feared that the British or French intended to seize his islands, Tyler issued a strong warning to European powers to keep away from Hawaii or risk creating "dissatisfaction on the part of the United States."

Tyler's crowning achievement in the diplomatic realm was ending the controversy between the United States and Great Britain over the boundary between Maine and Canadian New Brunswick. In 1838 settlers from Maine had pushed into the fertile Aroostook Valley, where they clashed in fistfights with lumbermen from New Brunswick, who also claimed this valley. Maine and New Brunswick then called out their militias, and Congress authorized President Van Buren to call for 50,000 soldiers in case a war with Great Britain should break out. The friction continued for several years, but neither country wanted to fight, so tempers were held in check until

Tyler's secretary of state could work out an agreement with British diplomats. The result of these efforts was the Webster-Ashburton Treaty of 1842, which divided the disputed territory and set the Maine–New Brunswick border.

In the same year, a different type of trouble developed in another part of New England. An uprising occurred in Rhode Island over that state's constitution, which gave voting rights only to men who owned a certain amount of land. Thomas Dorr, the leader of a group who could not vote, set up his own state government and undertook military preparations. These actions frightened the Rhode Island governor, and he called upon President Tyler for assistance. The president wished to see this dispute resolved without violence, but he made it clear that the national government would intervene if necessary to enforce that provision of the Constitution which makes state rebellions illegal. Tyler employed skill and patience in dealing with Dorr's Rebellion, and soon the people of Rhode Island adopted a new state constitution that liberalized voting qualifications.

Before he left the White House, Tyler was determined to bring Texas into the Union. The people in that huge territory had fought for their freedom from Mexico in 1836, and they were eager to have their land annexed by the United States. But serious obstacles lay in the way of annexation. The Mexican government refused to acknowledge the independence of Texas and threatened to go to war if the United States took it over. Also, many northerners did not want Texas to join the Union because it would add a vast new slave area to the nation. Some abolitionists, like former President John Quincy Adams, even maintained that if Texas were annexed, the states without slavery would be justified in leaving the Union.

President Tyler, however, felt that the acquisition of this large cotton-growing territory would increase immensely the wealth of the United States. He also feared that an independent Texas would form close ties with Great Britain. A Texas allied with the British could become a competing source of cotton and an important market for British manufactured goods.

Under the president's supervision, an annexation treaty was presented to the Senate, and Tyler urged its ratification on the grounds of broad national interest. But northern antislavery forces prevailed, and the Senate rejected the treaty in June 1844.

Convinced that large numbers of Americans wanted Texas to be annexed, Tyler decided to take his case to the people and run for reelection to the presidency. He knew he had no real chance to win a second term: the Whigs had disowned him, and the Democrats would not take back a president who had deserted their party. But both Martin Van Buren, who loomed as the potential 1844 Democratic nominee, and Henry Clay, the likely Whig standard-bearer, had announced their opposition to the immediate annexation of Texas. So Tyler declared he was an independent presidential candidate running under the banner of "Tyler and Texas!"

Tyler's entry into the contest was viewed with alarm by the delegates to the Democratic party convention as a possible threat to their capturing the southern states. Annexationists at the convention managed to prevent Van Buren from winning the nomination, which they gave instead to a "dark horse" candidate, James K. Polk of Tennessee. Polk favored the acquisition of Texas, and shortly after Polk's nomination Tyler dropped out of the race and threw his support to the Democratic contender.

Polk defeated Clay by a narrow margin, and Tyler interpreted his victory as a national mandate for admitting Texas to the Union. The outgoing president then asked both houses of Congress to pass a resolution calling for the annexation of Texas. (A congressional joint resolution requires only a majority vote, not the two-thirds margin needed for ratification of a treaty.) Congress acquiesced, and on March 1, 1845, two days before he left office, Tyler proudly signed the resolution. On his last day in office he signed a bill admitting Florida to the Union.

After Tyler left the presidency and retired to Sherwood Forest, he continued to play an active role in political matters. The former president was gravely concerned about the widening gulf between the North and the South. Following Abraham Lincoln's election to the presidency in 1860 and South Carolina's secession from the Union, Tyler made many speeches imploring both sides to avoid what appeared to be an inevitable war. He presided over a hastily called peace conference that met in secret session in Washington, D.C., for three weeks in February 1861. Delegates from seven slave states and fifteen free states attended the conference, but their last-ditch efforts failed to prevent hostilities.

Tyler was a member of the Virginia convention that voted to secede from the Union. Later he was elected to the Confederate Congress, thus becoming the only United States president to accept an office in the Confederate government. He went to Richmond to attend the first session, but died January 18, 1862, before the Congress assembled.

The United States government took no official notice of his death because our tenth president was considered a traitor to the Union. Nearly fifty years passed before Congress, in 1911, finally authorized the building of a monument to Tyler's memory in the Richmond cemetery where he was buried.

How capable a president was John Tyler? He did achieve some success in diplomatic ventures, and he spearheaded the drive to annex Texas, but his inability to persuade Congress to accept his leadership robbed him of any chance to leave his mark on important legislation. His implacable insistence on states' rights and his opposition to a national bank and higher tariffs kept him out of step with the party that had brought him to power. The Whigs, in their selfish desire to win southern votes, were clearly to blame for their foolhardy decision to run a man for vice president who opposed most of their major policies.

Nevertheless, Tyler did leave one indelible legacy: he established the tradition that vice presidents who succeed to the highest office in the land are full-fledged presidents, not merely acting presidents. The eight other vice presidents who later became accidental presidents had Tyler to thank for making certain that they would not be regarded as ineffectual figureheads in the White House.

Chapter 3
Millard Fillmore: From Log Cabin to White House

Nathaniel Fillmore worked hard to eke out a living from a small farm in Cayuga County, in northwestern New York. His large family lived in a crude log cabin that he had built with his own hands.

Millard, who was born in 1800, was the oldest son and the second of nine children. A strong boy, he did his share of farm jobs, clearing fields, planting and harvesting crops, and chopping wood. He attended school only a few months but managed to learn how to read and write. His father wanted him to acquire some trade, so when Millard was fourteen he became the indentured servant of a cloth maker. An indentured servant was somewhat like a slave because he was bound by a contract to work for an employer, who, in effect, owned him during the length of his contract. Millard was put to work preparing wool for spinning.

The ambitious youth had no intention of spending a long time as a wool carder; he was determined to get an education, which would open new doors of opportunity. He purchased a dictionary and mastered the definitions and spellings of many new words.

Millard did his daily tasks for the cloth maker quickly, and at the age of nineteen he enrolled as a part-time student at an academy in New Hope, New York. His teacher, Abigail Powers, was only twenty-one, and at first she felt awkward about teaching a pupil who was nearly the same age. But she was impressed by Millard's quest for knowledge and his speed in learning lessons. Within a short time Abigail introduced him to many subjects, including history, which he found fascinating. She also taught him geography and showed him the first map of the United States that he had ever seen. The handsome teenager—six feet tall, with wavy brown hair and blue eyes—grew very fond of his teacher, and eventually their friendship flowered into a romance.

Millard's studies progressed so swiftly that within a year he began studying law at the office of a judge. But legally he still was bound to work for the cloth maker. So to raise some money he spent part of his spare time teaching school and then bought up his indenture for $30.

For the next few years Millard continued his dual roles as a teacher and law student. In 1823 he was admitted to the bar and started practicing law in East Aurora, New York. Meanwhile, every chance that he had, he visited Abigail Powers. Finally, in 1826, seven years after they first met, Millard and Abigail were married. She continued teaching after their marriage, and even after the birth of the first of their two children. At that time it was unusual for a married woman with a child to hold down a job outside the home, but Abigail loved books and derived much satisfaction from using her teaching skills to educate and inspire young people.

In 1828 Fillmore ventured into the realm of

politics. He was elected to the first of three one-year terms in the New York State Assembly. His most important accomplishment in the state legislature was to secure the passage of a bill that abolished imprisonment for debt. While serving in the Assembly, he moved his family to Buffalo, New York, which was to become his home for the rest of his life.

Fillmore disliked the policies of President Andrew Jackson, and he was one of the founders of the Whig party in western New York. He was elected to the House of Representatives in 1832. Following one term in Congress he returned to his law practice in Buffalo. But spurred by his desire to advance the cause of the Whigs at the national level, he again sought a seat in Congress and was elected to the House of Representatives in 1836. He was then re-elected to two more terms. In 1841 Fillmore became chairman of the powerful House Ways and Means Committee, where he was instrumental in steering through the House the Tariff of 1842, which raised duties on foreign imports.

Even though his job in Washington, D.C., appeared secure, Fillmore decided to give it up and run for governor of New York in 1844. His opponent was a popular Democrat, Silas Wright, who had declined his party's nomination for the vice presidency because he had his eye instead on the governor's mansion at Albany. The election results were close: Wright defeated Fillmore by a margin of only about 10,000 votes out of the nearly half a million votes cast.

In 1847 Fillmore returned to the political arena and was elected comptroller of New York State. While holding this financial position, he worked to promote more trade through the Erie Canal.

As the presidential election of 1848 approached, voters realized they would be selecting a new president. Democrat James K. Polk, who then held the office, did not want a second term in the White House. He had achieved all of his major goals and was eager to step down from the presidency.

Much had happened during Polk's administration to change the boundaries of the United States. The dispute with Great Britain over land in the Pacific Northwest finally had been settled peacefully; the territory that would become the states of Oregon and Washington had been added to the United States. A much larger area in the Southwest had been acquired as a result of the Mexican War. Whether these newly won lands would permit slavery was a question that rekindled the old controversy between the North and the South.

For nearly thirty years, since the Missouri Compromise of 1820, there had been the same number of slave states and free states. But that fragile compromise would soon become unglued when the new territories applied for statehood. Southerners recognized that the climate of the Pacific Northwest would make slavery there unprofitable, but they were determined to allow slaves to be brought into the warmer lands, particularly California and New Mexico, that had been taken as prizes of war from Mexico.

Both political parties had southern and northern factions, and at their 1848 conventions they sought to play down the incendiary issue of slavery in the territories. The Democrats gave their presidential nomination to Senator Lewis Cass of Michigan and named as his running mate General William O. Butler of Kentucky. Even though he was not from the South, Cass's position on the extension of slavery was what he called "squatter sovereignty," which meant that the decision on slavery in a territory should be left to the voters who settled there.

Henry Clay, the perennial candidate of the Whigs, was now seventy-one years old but still eager to run again for the presidency. Many Whig leaders, however, did not agree that he should be the party's choice in 1848. Clay, they reasoned, already had been given enough chances to win the White House. Instead, they harked back to the 1840 election when the old war hero William Henry Harrison had provided the only Whig victory in a presidential race. It was time, they thought, to trot out another military man whose exploits on the battlefield would tug at the people's patriotic heartstrings.

Such a man was General Zachary Taylor, who had gained national adulation for winning important battles in the Mexican War. Although the log-cabin-and-hard-cider theme of 1840 could not be resurrected, there was a homespun, down-to-earth quality about Taylor that could appeal to many ordinary people. It was well known that when the general was commanding his troops, he seldom wore the elegant uniform of an officer; he much preferred to dress in baggy trousers and a wrinkled linen duster (a lightweight coatlike garment), and have on his head a floppy straw hat. Unlike Clay, he could not be accused of being a Washington wheeler-and-dealer. Taylor had never run for office before or even voted, and when asked about his political affiliation he surmised that he was probably a Whig but "not an ultra-Whig." And he had the endearing nickname of "Old Rough and Ready."

Taylor was a Louisiana slave owner, which pleased the southern Whigs. But he had never taken a strong stand in favor of extending slavery into the territories, which made him tolerable to many Whigs in the North. So the party handed Taylor its presidential nomination, notifying him of this high honor in a letter sent to his home in Baton Rouge, Louisiana. Even though Congress the previous year had authorized adhesive postage stamps, the letter was sent collect because postmasters were still accepting letters to be paid for by the recipient. At that time, however, Taylor was getting much unpaid mail and had instructed the local postmaster to send it all to the dead-letter office. Weeks passed, and the Whig chieftains wondered why their standard-bearer had not replied. Finally, they sent Taylor another letter, postage prepaid, and when "Old Rough and Ready" received it he quickly sent word that he accepted the presidential nomination.

Since they had named a southerner to head their ticket, the Whigs decided that his running mate should be an antislavery northerner who would balance the ticket and win them votes in the North. Millard Fillmore, the comptroller of New York, was not widely known outside his home state, but he met the requirements that his party laid down for the vice presidential candidate: he was a northerner who often had expressed his opposition to slavery. So, on the second ballot, the Whig convention selected Fillmore to run with Taylor.

The Whigs did not adopt a party platform, and their campaign centered on Taylor's war record and agreeable personality, not on the slavery issue that threatened to tear the country apart. Party leaders were delighted that their presidential nominee took no strong preelection stands on any questions that might lose him votes. Abraham Lincoln, an Illinois Whig congressman, approved of Taylor's vagueness on issues, declaring:

> The people say to General Taylor, "If you are elected, shall we have a national bank?" He answers. "Your will, gentlemen, not mine." "What about the tariff?" "Say yourselves."

"Shall our rivers and harbors be improved?"
"Just as you please. If you desire a bank,
an alteration of the tariff, internal
improvements, any or all, I will not hinder
you. If you do not desire them, I will not
attempt to force them on you. . . ." [1]

Not all Americans were favorably impressed by the devious ways in which both Taylor and Democratic candidate Cass evaded the pressing problem of whether slavery would be allowed in the territories. Three months before the election, some antislavery leaders in both the Democratic and Whig parties formed a new third party, the Free-Soilers, which was dedicated to the principle that there should be no extension of slavery. Former Democratic President Martin Van Buren was the presidential candidate of the Free-Soil party, and the vice presidential nomination went to Charles Francis Adams of Massachusetts, a former Whig and the son of former President John Quincy Adams.

The election was very close, with Taylor and Cass each winning 127 electoral votes, not counting the largest state, New York. The Free-Soil party carried no state, but it won over 26 percent of the votes cast in New York. This strong showing of the Free-Soilers in New York hurt Cass's chances to win that state. The Whigs, on the other hand, had an advantage in New York because it was Fillmore's home state and he was popular with voters there. New York's 36 electoral votes were captured by the Whigs, thus enabling the Taylor-Fillmore ticket to eke out a narrow victory.

Vice President Fillmore presided over the Senate during one of the most critical periods in American history. There were several sources of bitter sectional strife, all involving slavery. One of the most urgent problems was what to do about California, whose settlers were clamoring for admission to the Union as a free state. Northern senators heartily approved California's admission, but their southern colleagues were firmly opposed to upsetting the delicate balance between free states and slave states established by the Missouri Compromise. Feelings on both sides grew so tense that some lawmakers attended sessions armed with pistols and bowie knives.

In December 1849 President Taylor startled Congress and the nation by announcing that he favored the immediate statehood of California. This surprised and enraged southerners, who assailed slaveholder Taylor for deserting their ranks. Their charges of betrayal were accompanied by threats of secession and possible civil war.

To deal with this alarming situation, Senator Henry Clay proposed a compromise embodied in a series of measures designed to balance northern and southern demands. The chief provisions favoring the North were that California be admitted as a free state and that the slave trade, but not slavery itself, be prohibited in the District of Columbia. The South, in turn, would gain a more powerful Fugitive Slave Law, making it easier for southerners to capture runaway slaves. The question of slavery in the New Mexico territory would be resolved by a vote of the people who settled there. And an argument over the Texas–New Mexico border would be settled by Texas's ceding some land to New Mexico and receiving money from the federal government to compensate for its loss.

President Taylor of course agreed with Clay's proposal that California become a state, but he opposed other parts of the compromise, declaring that the slavery question should not be decided by the federal government. Outraged southerners then sent representatives to a meeting in Nashville to discuss secession, should California be admitted and their demand for a tougher Fugitive Slave Law be ignored. Meanwhile, slaveholders in Texas resisted Clay's measure to cede land to New Mexico, which probably would forbid slavery. The Texas government threatened to send 2,500 soldiers to defend its border with New Mexico. Taylor replied that federal troops would be used to prevent Texas from attacking in the disputed area.

Month after month while the Senate debated what later was called the Compromise of 1850, Vice President Fillmore gave no indication of how he felt about Clay's measures. Courteous and dignified, he sat in the front of the Senate chamber, rapping his gavel again and again to try to bring order in a house erupting with emotional outbursts. As the time for voting drew near, the vice president tried to estimate the number of yes and no ballots that would be cast. It would be an extremely close decision, he surmised, possibly even a tie, which would require that he cast the deciding vote.

Fillmore knew that the president opposed the compromise, so in early July he paid Taylor a visit to explain his position. He told his superior that if the vote were to deadlock, "and if I should feel it my duty to vote for it, as I might, I wished him to understand that it was not out of any hostility to him or his Administration, but the vote would be given because I deemed it for the interests of the country."[2]

A few days later, on a hot, steamy Fourth of July, Taylor attended a lengthy ceremony for the dedication of the new Washington Monument. When he returned to the White House, the president consumed huge quantities of iced milk and cherries. That night he was seized with violent cramps, and on the evening of July 9 he died from what was probably acute gastroenteritis.

Fillmore issued a brief statement of condolence and then sent the Senate a note saying he no longer would be its presiding officer. At that time the position of president pro tempore (temporary president) of the Senate was vacant, and Fillmore urged the senators to fill this office immediately because the person who held it would be next in line to succeed to the presidency. The Senate dutifully elected William R. King of Alabama president pro tempore. He was a Democrat, so if Fillmore had died in the presidency, the White House would have been lost by the Whigs.

Following Taylor's death, no one questioned whether Fillmore would be the actual president or merely the acting president, as had happened when John Tyler faced a similar situation. At noon on July 10, 1850, Millard Fillmore took the presidential oath in the hall of the House of Representatives in the presence of both houses of Congress.

The *Daily National Intelligencer*, in its July 11 issue, described how the accession of the vice president to the full power of the presidency was, by 1850, taken for granted:

> *The death of the President being announced, a citizen,*
> *plainly attired, enters among the assembled*
> *Representatives of the Nation, walks up to the Clerk's*
> *desk, takes an oath on the Bible to support the*
> *Constitution of the United States; and, by this*
> *brief ceremony, he becomes, in an instant of time,*
> *invested with the command of the whole military*
> *force of a mighty empire, with the execution of*
> *its laws and the administration of the power.*
> *No one objects or dreams of objection; the act*
> *is acquiesced in as a thing of course, and with*

the submission that would be rendered to a law
of nature. The scepter of the People passes
into his hands as quietly and as quickly as a
power of attorney could be acknowledged before
a justice of the peace.[3]

The members of Taylor's cabinet all tendered their resignations to the new president. Fillmore accepted them but asked these men to remain in their positions for a month until he could assemble his administration. They agreed to remain for only one week. So one of the president's first tasks was to fill the cabinet vacancies, and for these positions he sought persons with a "national outlook," who would not favor either the North or the South. He appointed as secretary of state Daniel Webster, who resigned his Senate seat to take the same office in the executive department that he had held in the administrations of Harrison and Tyler. Although a northerner who detested slavery, Webster had fought on the Senate floor for the Compromise of 1850, including its stronger Fugitive Slave Law, because it seemed to offer the best chance for reaching a truce between North and South.

Meanwhile, Abigail Fillmore was busy moving her family into the White House. She soon discovered, much to her displeasure, that the executive mansion had no books, not even a Bible. Mrs. Fillmore then persuaded her husband to get a modest appropriation from Congress to start the first White House library. Also, mindful of how much work was involved in carrying bath water by hand, she had water pipes and a zinc bathtub installed in the White House.[4]

Cast-iron stoves were then coming into vogue, replacing the open fireplaces that for centuries had been used for cooking. Mrs. Fillmore ordered one of these new stoves for the White House kitchen. When

49

it arrived, the family cook, bewildered by its array of drafts and pulleys, refused to try out the stove. This domestic crisis was not resolved until the president himself went to the U.S. Patent Office, studied a model and the directions for using the stove, and then taught the cook how to operate it.[5]

Shortly after Fillmore became president, Congress passed each of the bills that composed the Compromise of 1850. One by one the president signed them into law. He did hesitate when the bill pertaining to fugitive slaves reached his desk and asked the attorney general to assure him that it was constitutional. Mrs. Fillmore cautioned her husband that signing this highly controversial bill would bring about his political suicide. Fillmore personally disliked the measure, but, after the attorney general reported that it did not violate the Constitution, the president put his signature to it.

Mrs. Fillmore's forecast was correct: the Fugitive Slave Act caused such a furor among antislavery forces that the president lost his northern base of support and thus any chance to win a second term. Political observers who had been surprised when slave owner Zachary Taylor called for the admission of California as a free state, now were dumbfounded to learn that Fillmore had gone in the opposite direction: a long-standing opponent of slavery, he had endorsed an act that would make it a crime not to return slaves to the masters they deserted. Furthermore, Fillmore threatened to use troops to enforce the Fugitive Slave Act, sternly declaring that northerners, as well as southerners, had to live up to their constitutional obligations.

Except for the Compromise of 1850, there was no important legislation passed during Fillmore's term. The president, however, did attain modest successes on the international scene. He authorized a special expedition led by Commodore Matthew C. Perry to Japan, a country that had remained virtually isolated from the Western world. The small American fleet stayed in Tokyo harbor only ten days, but a message from Fillmore to the Japanese ruler expressed the sincere desire of the United States to trade with his country. An official trade treaty was not signed until after Fillmore left office, but he took pride in opening the door to Western contacts with a major country in Asia.

During Fillmore's White House tenure, a band of Americans was preparing to sail to Cuba, then a colony of Spain, and stage a rebellion against the Spanish authorities in Havana. The rebels were mainly southerners who wanted to take over Cuba and make it an American outpost supported by slave labor. Fillmore issued a presidential proclamation ordering this group not to invade Cuba, but the insurrectionists sailed for the island anyway. Their uprising failed, and some of the invaders were executed by the Spanish government. News of the executions caused anti-Spanish riots at New Orleans and the wrecking of the Spanish consulate there. President Fillmore was pressured to take action against Spain, but he refused to retaliate for an uprising that he felt was illegal and unjust.

In 1852 Fillmore sought renomination at the Whig convention, and ironically most of the support for the president from New York came from southern delegates, who appreciated his endorsement of the Compromise of 1850. His chief opponent was General Winfield Scott, another Mexican War hero. The two major rivals had nearly equal strength, and Fillmore led Scott on the first ballot by a single vote, 133–132, with a third contender, Daniel Webster, polling 29 votes. Neither of the front-runners would defer to the other, so a tense battle ensued for three long days and fifty-three ballots. Finally, Scott won, receiving 159 votes compared with 112 for Fillmore and 21 for Webster.

The Democrats had assembled two weeks earlier than the Whigs, and their convention also was divisive and drawn out. The weary delegates cast forty-nine ballots before they nominated a little-known candidate for the presidency, former Senator Franklin Pierce of New Hampshire.

In the November election Pierce won a landslide victory; Scott carried only four states. This disastrous defeat shocked the Whigs so badly that it started the gradual disintegration of their party.

When Fillmore's term ended, the president and his wife looked forward to returning to Buffalo and then traveling abroad. But Mrs. Fillmore never left Washington. At the inauguration of Pierce, on a cold, blustery day, she stood on the windswept portico of the Capitol and contracted a chill. Soon she developed pneumonia and, less than one month later, died in a Washington hotel.

Four years later Fillmore wanted to resume his political career. By this time the political landscape had changed drastically: the Whig party was nearly dead, and it had been replaced by two new groups, the Republican and the American parties. Many former Whigs, including Abraham Lincoln, had joined the Republican party. Fillmore, perhaps foolishly, cast his lot with the American, or "Know-Nothing," party as a possible vehicle for his comeback.

The nickname of "Know-Nothings" came about because members of the party were instructed to reply "I know nothing" whenever they were asked what their party stood for. But it was no secret that the Know-Nothings were fervently opposed to aliens and Catholics. Their chief goal was to place severe restrictions on the large number of European immigrants who had arrived in the 1840s and 1850s.

52

In 1856 Fillmore accepted the presidential nomination of the American party, and his running mate was Andrew Jackson Donelson of Tennessee. Fillmore later also was nominated by the remnants of the Whig party.

The nativist platform of the American party on which Fillmore ran contained these inflammatory words: *"Americans must rule America; and to this end native-born citizens should be selected for all state, federal, and municipal offices of government employment, in preference to all others."*[6] Another plank of their party platform demanded that the naturalization period for immigrants be extended to twenty-one years.

Fillmore's rivals for the presidency were Democrat James Buchanan and John C. Fremont, the first presidential nominee of the Republican party. In the popular vote results, Buchanan had 1,836,072 votes to Fremont's 1,342,345 and Fillmore's 873,053. Buchanan carried nineteen states with 174 electoral votes, while Fremont, who did not run in the South, captured a surprising eleven states with 114 electoral votes. Fillmore won only the state of Maryland and its eight electoral votes. Even so, the sentiment against immigrants in the 1850s must have been intense, or Fillmore would not have polled nearly a million votes out of about 4 million that were cast.

Following their defeat in 1856, the Know-Nothings quickly disappeared from the national scene, and Fillmore devoted most of his time to civic affairs in Buffalo. In 1858 he married a wealthy widow, Caroline Carmichael McIntosh. They purchased a mansion on Niagara Square in Buffalo, where they lived quietly together until Fillmore's death in 1874 at the age of seventy-four.

Why has Millard Fillmore never been regarded as one of our stronger presidents? The answer lies largely in his support of the Fugitive Slave Act, which blatantly appeased the South and its institution of slavery, and in his lack of bold, creative leadership during one of the most turbulent periods in American history. The Fugitive Slave Act hounded Fillmore for the rest of his life and into history. Although he had worked for the Union cause during the Civil War, a mob vandalized the outside of Fillmore's home after Abraham Lincoln was assassinated.

Still, an argument can be made in defense of the course of action Fillmore took while president. He begrudgingly accepted the Fugitive Slave Act as an integral part of a broad compromise designed to avert the war that ultimately began in 1861. The Compromise of 1850 postponed this war for more than a decade. While the uneasy truce prevailed, the North grew stronger economically and militarily—making it much more able to combat the tragic effort of the southern states to secede from the Union.

Chapter 4
Andrew Johnson:
President on Trial

Like Millard Fillmore, Andrew Johnson was an indentured servant in his youth. Born in a wooden shack in Raleigh, North Carolina, in 1808, Andrew came from a poverty-stricken family. His father, a janitor, died when the boy was three; his mother remarried but she had to continue working as a hotel maid. When Andrew was fourteen, his mother bound him and his older brother, William, to a local tailor.

Andrew Johnson never had the opportunity to attend school. But the apprentice tailors were read to as they worked, and Andrew soon became fascinated by books and thirsted for more knowledge. He knew that to become an educated person he must be able to read, so he undertook the painstaking task of teaching himself this skill.

After working two years as indentured servants, the Johnson brothers fled from their employer. The angered tailor immediately placed an ad in the Raleigh newspaper, offering a $10 reward for the return of the runaways. Andrew wandered south until he reached Carthage, North Carolina, about 75 miles from Raleigh. There he worked awhile in a tailor shop before moving on to Laurens, South Carolina.

When he was eighteen, Andrew slipped back into Raleigh. But he knew he couldn't stay there long because the tailor to whom he was still legally bound could force his indentured servant to work for him until he turned twenty-one. So Andrew, together with his mother and stepfather, decided to head west. They packed all their belongings in a two-wheel open cart drawn by a half-blind pony. Slowly they scaled the Blue Ridge Mountains. After a month of traveling and sleeping outdoors every night, they finally reached the poor mountain town of Greeneville, in eastern Tennessee. Learning that the elderly town tailor had recently retired, Andrew rented a cabin and opened his own shop under the sign "A. Johnson, Tailor."

Andrew felt comfortable and at ease with most of his neighbors in Greeneville. Like himself, they worked hard with their hands—as farmers, bricklayers, carpenters, cobblers, and blacksmiths. These plain people treated Andrew as their equal. This was vastly different from the situation he had left in North Carolina, where Andrew and his family had been looked down upon by the planter aristocracy, who scorned them and called them "poor white trash."

Shortly after arriving in Greeneville, Andrew met and fell in love with Eliza McCardle. She was the daughter of a local cobbler, who had died when Eliza was a young child. Andrew was eighteen and Eliza only sixteen when they married. (He was married younger than any other president; she was married younger than any other First Lady.) They became the parents of two daughters and three sons. Andrew was nineteen when their first child, Martha, was born, and nearly forty-four at the time that their youngest son, Andrew, Jr., was born.

Eliza was better educated than Andrew, and she frequently tutored her husband. Under her guidance, he improved his reading and learned how to write and do math problems. They used his tailor shop as a classroom, and while he cut cloth and sewed garments, Eliza often read aloud to him.

Andrew Johnson's shop also became the site of heated political discussions. The other townsfolk were impressed by the dedication and zeal with which the young tailor promoted the interests of the laboring class. They first elected him a town alderman and later, in 1831, the mayor of Greeneville.

Johnson's reputation as a leader of working men and women spread beyond the confines of his hometown. In 1835 he was elected to the Tennessee House of Representatives, and in 1841 to the state Senate.

Continuing to climb the political ladder, in 1843 Democrat Johnson became the first tradesman or mechanic from a slave state to win a seat in the United States House of Representatives. He held this position ten years and proved himself to be an able and energetic congressman. Ever mindful of his lack of a formal education, Johnson would read late into the night, gathering all the facts pertinent to the bills the House was considering.

In an age noted for florid oratory, the tailor from Greeneville practiced and perfected his public speaking. Although his speeches did not contain the graceful style and literary references expressed by some of his better-educated colleagues, they were nevertheless direct, forceful, and effective. A *New York Times* reporter said that in his speeches Johnson "cut and slashed right and left, tore big wounds and left something behind to fester and remember. His phraseology may be uncouth, but his views are easily understood and he talks strong thoughts and carefully culled facts in quick succession."[1]

Johnson strongly supported national interests as opposed to states' rights. This antagonized many aristocratic southern legislators, who regarded him as a loathsome hillbilly experienced only in the crude, lowly ways of a manual laborer. But the outspoken congressman was proud of having advanced "by the sweat of his brow." Once, when he was insulted because of his humble background on the floor of the House, he retorted angrily, "I do not forget that I am a mechanic. I am proud to own it. Neither do I forget that Adam was a tailor and sewed fig leaves, or that our Saviour was the son of a carpenter."[2]

In 1853 Johnson was elected governor of Tennessee. At his inauguration, the man whom newspapers called "the Mechanic Governor" refused to ride in a carriage. He said he wanted to walk to the Nashville Capitol, as the poor people who supported him did. During his two terms in the statehouse, he established Tennessee's first public school system, a state library, and a regular program of agricultural and mechanical fairs.

Elected to the United States Senate in 1857, at a time when the North and South were drifting toward war, Johnson did not give his complete support to either side. Since he owned a few black slaves and did not oppose the institution of slavery, he urged northerners to comply with the Fugitive Slave Act and argued that Congress did not have the power to restrict the spread of slavery. In the 1860 presidential election, which Republican Abraham Lincoln won, Johnson voted for John C. Breckinridge, the candidate of the southern Democrats. On the other hand, Johnson agreed with the position held by many northerners that the southern states should not, un-

58

der any circumstances, be permitted to secede from the Union.

Johnson's most notable accomplishment as a senator was sponsoring the Homestead Act, which opened the public lands of the West to the small farmers whose cause he championed. By this act, 160 acres of western land were made available to the head of any family that would settle on this land for five years.

Shortly after Lincoln's election, southern states began seceding from the Union, and their representatives in Congress packed their bags and went home. When Johnson learned that the voters of Tennessee were going to hold an election to determine whether their state would go with the Confederacy or stay with the Union, he hurried home to plead with his constituents not to let Tennessee secede.

En route home Johnson's train had to pass through Virginia, where the sentiment for secession was strong and growing violent. At one stop a mob forced its way onto the train and lunged toward Johnson. He drew his revolver and threatened to shoot anyone who touched him. In Lynchburg, Virginia, another mob waited, this time with a rope to hang him. With his gun pointed into the crowd, Johnson stood on the train steps challenging the secessionists to come get him.

Even back in Tennessee, Johnson was rebuked again and again for deserting his southern brothers. He did find some support in the eastern mountainous area from which he came, and after the war started, this part of the Volunteer State supplied about 35,000 soldiers for the Union cause. But when the votes in the statewide plebiscite had been counted, the people of Tennessee had decided, by nearly a two-to-one margin, to cast their lot with the Confederacy. Johnson was crestfallen, but perhaps the cruelest blow to his pride was a banner waving above the main street of Greeneville that read ANDREW JOHNSON, TRAITOR.

While Johnson was called a traitor and hanged in effigy in his native South, the senator from Tennessee was hailed as a courageous hero by northerners. After hostilities between the North and South began, he was the lone southerner to remain in the Senate. When he addressed his colleagues about the Union's war aims, Johnson declared:

> *This war is not prosecuted on our part in any spirit of oppression, nor for any purpose of conquest or subjugation, nor for the purpose of overthrowing or interfering with the rights or established institutions of those states, but to defend and maintain the supremacy of the Constitution and all laws made in pursuance thereof, and to preserve the Union, with all the dignity, equality, and rights of the several states unimpaired.*[3]

His explanation that the war was not being fought to interfere with the "established institutions" of the South was a reference to slavery. Clearly Johnson did not believe that the North had taken up arms to free the black slaves. This was consistent with President Lincoln's beliefs at that time; it was not until January 1863, nearly two years after the war started, that Lincoln issued his Emancipation Proclamation, and it applied only to freeing slaves behind Confederate lines.

Early in 1862 the Union forces under General Ulysses S. Grant seized Nashville and part of western Tennessee. Then, at Lincoln's request, Johnson gave up his Senate seat to become military governor of Tennessee with the rank of brigadier general. Johnson was instructed to reestablish federal authority in the state and maintain peace and order until such time as a civil government could be restored. The military governor moved forcefully to carry out his orders. He had fortifications built near Nashville, impressed slaves into the Union army, dismissed officeholders who would not pledge allegiance to the federal government, suspended anti-Union newspapers, and even arrested clergymen who spoke for the Confederacy from their pulpits. Several times, southern soldiers laid siege to Nashville, but they were unable to retake the city or capture its brave commander.

As the war dragged on with no clear resolution in sight, many northerners became frustrated with Lincoln's leadership. Some wanted him to be bolder and more aggressive. Others argued that the horrendous war with its staggering number of casualties—all Americans—must be brought to an end. Let the southern states go, they pleaded, so that peace could return to the ravaged land.

By the summer of 1864, when the political parties met in conventions to choose their presidential and vice presidential candidates, the Republicans knew that Lincoln's popularity was at low ebb. There was so much dissatisfaction with his conduct of the war that his reelection was in serious doubt. Still, the Union cause could not be deserted simply to appease those northerners who were tired of the stalemated war.

So the Republican chieftains adopted a strategy to reach out to the so-called War Democrats, voters who considered themselves Democrats but whose first priority was that the North must win the war to save the Union. The name Republican was dropped by the party for this one election, and in its place was substituted a new name—the National Union party.

Then Lincoln's supporters took an even bolder step to appeal for Democratic votes: they decided not to run Vice President Hannibal Hamlin of Maine for a second term. Instead, they gave the nomination to Andrew Johnson, a War Democrat—a southerner who had owned slaves but a loyal Unionist. This was the only time in American history when either major political party selected a candidate for vice president from the other party.

The Democratic party platform called for an immediate end to the hostilities and a negotiated peace. The party's candidate for president was General George B. McClellan, who had been commander of the Union forces until President Lincoln demoted him for not being sufficiently aggressive. McClellan accepted the nomination but refused to call the war a failure, thus defying those Democrats who sought peace at any price.

The election was expected to be very close, and Lincoln was gravely concerned that he would not be given a second term in the White House. Shortly before Election Day, however, the northern armies won some major battles, which boosted the chances of the Lincoln-Johnson ticket because many northerners became convinced that victory for their side was now in sight. When the votes were counted, the National Union party had reelected its Republican president and elected its Democratic vice presidential candidate by a substantial majority.

At the time of his inauguration, Johnson was recovering from an attack of typhoid fever. Feeling weak and nauseous when he entered the stuffy Senate chamber, the vice president-elect drank some whiskey. He thought the liquor would fortify him; instead, it made him appear drunk. When called on to speak, he slurred his words and the remarks he made were repetitious, rambling, almost incoherent. The audience was aghast, and Senator Charles Sumner of Massachusetts decried Johnson's speech as the "most unfortunate thing that has occurred in our history."[4]

President Lincoln was embarrassed by the incident, but it did not shake his faith in the vice president. "I have known Andy Johnson for many years," he later told a friend. "He made a bad slip the other day, but you need not be scared, Andy ain't a drunkard."[5]

Shortly after the inauguration of Lincoln and Johnson, General Grant accepted the surrender of General Robert E. Lee's southern army at Appomattox Courthouse in Virginia. The long, costly Civil War finally was drawing to a close, and President Lincoln faced the difficult task of restoring a nation that had been split into two irreconcilable sections. In his Second Inaugural Address, Lincoln expressed his fervent wish that the war would be followed by a merciful, charitable peace. "With malice toward none," he stated, "with charity for all, . . . let us strive . . . to bind up the nation's wounds. . . ." He maintained that, as soon as possible, the southern states should be functioning again within the reconstructed Union. The president also recognized that slavery must be abolished, but he suggested no measures to guarantee the former slaves' civil rights, including the precious right to vote.

Some northerners in Congress disagreed sharply with Lincoln's moderate views about Reconstruction. Called the Radical Republicans, they believed that the defiant South should not be treated leniently. They were appalled by the carnage inflicted by the Confederates on Union soldiers: 360,000 dead, another 275,000 wounded. These staggering losses, the Radical Republicans insisted, must be avenged. The South must be treated like any other defeated country, and those who had fought for the Confederacy must be stripped of all powers and denied the vote. Moreover, the freed slaves must be helped economically and given all the rights of other citizens.

The argument over Reconstruction between Lincoln and the Radical Republicans had not been resolved before the president fell victim to a conspiracy of Confederate sympathizers and was assassinated at Ford's Theater. That same fateful night, April 14, 1865, Vice President Johnson also was targeted for assassination by another of the conspirators. George Atzerodt, the would-be murderer, took a room in a Washington hotel just above the suite where Johnson was staying. His instructions were to knock on Johnson's door and then shoot the vice president at precisely the same time that John Wilkes Booth was murdering Lincoln. But at the last moment Atzerodt apparently lost his nerve and fled from the hotel on horseback. He was later captured and hanged.

Forty-one days after he had become vice president, Andrew Johnson took his oath of office as the nation's chief executive. At first the Radical Republicans thought the new president was in their camp. He had publicly declared that no punishment could be too severe for the traitors in the vanquished South, and that Jefferson Davis, president of the Confederacy, should be hanged.

Soon, however, President Johnson announced that when he had demanded that traitors be punished, he had in mind the group of wealthy plantation owners he had always despised. Otherwise, his plan for Reconstruction was very similar to Lincoln's. He called for each southern state to hold a convention in which it repealed its acts related to secession, repudiated debts brought about by the war, and ratified the Thirteenth Amendment, which gave freedom to the slaves. After these steps were taken, the states would be readmitted to the Union and could elect local officials, congressmen, and senators.

Leaders of the Radical Republicans warned Johnson that his plan for restoring the Union was much too soft on the white southerners and did nothing to protect the rights of the South's black people. But Congress was not then in session, and the president moved quickly to put his policies into operation. By December, when Congress assembled again, every Confederate state except Texas had met the Reconstruction qualifications and had elected its local officeholders and representatives to both houses of Congress.

Prodded by the Radical Republicans, Congress refused to admit the newly elected senators and representatives from the reorganized southern states. Then the Senate and House of Representatives formed a fifteen-member Joint Committee on Reconstruction to establish a congressional program for dealing with the South, which promised to be vastly different from the president's plan. The Capitol and the White House now were at war over the course that Reconstruction would take.

The Radical Republicans shot off an opening salvo by passing a bill extending the life of the Freedmen's Bureau, a War Department agency that tried to help the former slaves acquire food, clothing, jobs, medical care, and educational facilities. It also attempted to protect the civil rights of southern blacks and to see that employers treated them fairly. President Johnson vetoed the bill, declaring that since the southern states had as yet no United States senators or representatives, the federal government could not pass laws affecting them. Also, he objected to the Freedmen's Bureau because it was a military tribunal and not a civilian agency, and he expressed the fear that the bureau was making the ex-slaves wards of the nation.

Supporters of the Freedmen's Bureau bill could not muster the two-thirds vote in both houses of Congress needed to override the president's veto. Frustrated by the will of the man in the White House, the enraged Radical Republicans lashed out at Johnson for being a southerner, a former slave owner, a Democrat. They accused him of sympathizing with the Confederate rebels, and a few even dared to suggest that he might have been involved in the plot to assassinate Lincoln. Newspapers in the North referred to Johnson as the "drunken tailor," and Johnson's popularity with the voters who had elected him vice president sharply declined.

Later the Freedmen's Bureau bill was passed again, and this time the president's veto was overridden. Then the Radical Republicans passed a sweeping civil rights bill, promising blacks the protection of their rights in federal courts. Johnson vetoed it on the grounds that it violated states' rights, but Congress overrode his veto.

The next item on the Radical Republicans' agenda was to propose the Fourteenth Amendment to the Constitution. This important amendment said that a state may not "deprive any person of life, liberty, or property without due process of law, nor deny to any person within its jurisdiction the equal protection of the law." Another section of the amendment would deprive the southern states of their full representation in Congress and the Electoral College if they forbade black males to vote. The Fourteenth Amendment also excluded from public office all ex-Confederates who previously had held any government position that required them to take an oath to support the United States Constitution, unless they were pardoned by a vote of both houses of Congress.

The president cannot veto a constitutional amendment, but Johnson vigorously opposed that part of the Fourteenth Amendment which prohibited southerners from electing to office former Confederates who had not been pardoned by Congress. The president urged the southern states to reject the amendment; this unfortunate advice lost him even more of his dwindling support in the North.

Developments in the South further infuriated the Radical Republicans. The new governments in the southern states were passing laws designed to continue white supremacy. Blacks were not allowed to vote or serve on juries. No provisions were made for blacks to go to school and obtain an education that could enable them to hold higher-paying jobs. Southern legislators passed special laws known as "Black Codes" to keep the former slaves under tight control. These laws ordered blacks to make long-term contracts with employers; those without such contracts could be arrested as vagrants and their labor sold to the highest bidder. In some instances they were even bound over to work for their former masters. The postwar South apparently paid only lip service to the Thirteenth Amendment abolishing slavery and intended to treat the black population permanently as a subservient lower class.

In the first round of his battle against the Radical Republicans, Johnson generally had stayed inside the White House, attacking his enemies with scornful veto messages and curt written statements to the press. During those days the president's manner, which had seldom been lighthearted before, now was grim and combative. Almost always dressed in a black suit, he appeared to be in constant mourning. Touches of gray peppered his black hair and bushy eyebrows. His unhappy attitude was reflected in his brooding dark eyes and a scowl that usually creased his forehead. He worked ceaselessly at his desk, rarely taking any time for recreation, except for an occasional game of checkers.

Family concerns contributed to Johnson's despondent mood. During the Civil War his oldest son, Charles, had died in Union uniform after a fall from a horse. The husband of one of his daughters, Mary, had been killed fighting against the Confederates. Another son, Robert, had served as a colonel in the Tennessee Union Cavalry, but he returned from war an alcoholic. He was private secretary to his father during his tenure as president, but Robert Johnson died at age thirty-five, less than two months after his father left the White House.

The president was very worried about the failing health of his wife, Eliza. She suffered from tuberculosis and was an invalid. The little entertaining that occurred in the president's home was supervised by Martha Patterson, the Johnsons' oldest daughter. When she assumed her social duties as White House hostess, Mrs. Patterson remarked: "We are plain people from the mountains of Tennessee called here for a short time by a national calamity. I trust too much will not be expected of us."[6]

When the 1866 congressional elections neared, the president decided to take his case to the people and plead with them not to elect more Radical Republicans to Congress. He embarked on a long tour, described as a "swing around the circle," and visited several large cities, including Baltimore, Philadelphia, New York, Chicago, Cincinnati, and Pittsburgh. Large crowds greeted him nearly every place he spoke. Some listeners were sympathetic and applauded his remarks. Others would boo and hiss him, laugh loudly when he tried to make a serious point, call out that he was a traitor, and goad the president to lose his temper. Then the enraged Johnson, disregarding the dignity of the office he held, would strike back furiously, shouting wild, crude, personal insults at his enemies in Congress.

Johnson's "swing around the circle" was a total disaster for the distraught president. The congressional elections that he had sought to influence went against him: Radical Republicans increased their numbers in Congress, putting them firmly in control of Reconstruction. Moreover, the nasty slurs that Johnson had aimed at his opponents in his speeches heightened their determination to humble him.

In 1867 and 1868, Congress passed a series of four acts establishing military rule and harsh conditions of readmission for the southern states. Johnson vetoed all these measures, but each time Congress overrode the president's disapproval.

The struggle between Johnson and the Radical Republicans reached a climax in 1868 when the president was tried on impeachment charges. The previous year Congress had passed the Tenure of Office Act over Johnson's veto. This law forbade the president to remove, without the consent of the Senate, any officeholder whose appointment had required Senate approval. It was actually a trap set to snare the president for violating a law, thus making him subject to removal from office on the grounds that he had committed a crime.

Johnson tumbled into this trap after he asked for the resignation of Secretary of War Edwin M. Stanton, who he learned was secretly in league with the Radical Republicans and trying to undermine his administration. When Stanton refused to resign, Johnson first suspended him and later dismissed him. The president said he had done nothing illegal in firing Stanton; the Tenure of Office Act, he was certain, was unconstitutional. (The act was repealed, in large part, in 1887 and declared unconstitutional by the Supreme Court in 1926.) Furthermore, Johnson maintained that this act could not pertain to his dismissal of Stanton, since Lincoln, not he, had appointed Stanton to the cabinet.

Although the president insisted that the constitutionality of the Tenure of Office Act first must be determined by the courts, the Radical Republicans in the House of Representatives brushed aside this notion and instead drew up eleven impeachment counts against Johnson. In a presidential impeachment trial, members of the lower house of Congress prosecute the case, the Senate acts as the jury, and the chief justice of the Supreme Court is the presiding judge. To remove the president from office, the Senate must vote for conviction by at least a two-thirds margin.

Andrew Johnson was the only president of the United States tried for impeachment. (Richard Nixon faced impeachment charges voted by the House of Representatives, but he resigned from the presidency before the trial could begin.) The Johnson trial was the most famous and one of the most dramatic trials in American history. Huge crowds gathered outside the Capitol, spectators packed the galleries, and streams of reporters rushed from the Senate chamber to relay news of the important trial to an anxious public.

The first eight articles of impeachment charged the president with intent and conspiracy to violate the Constitution and the Tenure of Office Act. The ninth accused him of violating an army appropriations act. The tenth charged him with behavior that disgraced Congress, including delivering some speeches "in a loud voice." The eleventh article summarized the first ten; Johnson's foes and friends agreed that it was the key article that would determine the president's guilt or innocence.

For two months the prosecution and defense attorneys argued the case. Finally, on May 16, 1868, the Senate began to ballot on article eleven. There were fifty-four senators at the time; thirty-six votes were needed for conviction. The Radical Republicans felt certain they had thirty-five votes; the defense was sure of twelve. That left seven senators—all Republicans—who were not committed. The prosecution needed the vote of only one of these seven doubtful senators to drive the president from office.

Tension heightened every time one of the uncommitted Republican senators rose to announce his decision. One by one, all seven voted "not guilty." The final count on the eleventh article of impeachment was 35–19 in favor of conviction—one vote short of the necessary two-thirds majority. Ten days later Johnson was acquitted of two other articles by the same margin; the other articles were never brought to a vote.

The seven Republican senators who had defied their leaders and voted "not guilty" knew that their stand was so unpopular that it probably meant the end of their political careers. When they returned to their home states, they were subjected to various forms of abuse, from nasty jeers and dangerous threats to hangings in effigy. None of them was reelected to the Senate.

But these courageous senators helped establish an important precedent: a president cannot be removed from office simply because his political views are not the same as those of the persons who control Congress. Senator Lyman Trumbull of Illinois, one of the seven Republicans who voted for Johnson, said that if a president can be found guilty of impeachment charges when there is ". . . insufficient cause, no future President will be safe who happens to differ with a majority of the House and two-thirds of the Senate on any measure deemed by them important. . . . What then becomes of the checks and balances of the Constitution so carefully devised and so vital to its perpetuity? They are all gone."[7]

Like John Tyler and Millard Fillmore, the two accidental presidents who preceded him to the White House, Johnson had little opportunity to sponsor major legislation because an antagonistic Congress paid scant attention to his requests. Also like Tyler and Fillmore, Johnson had to look to foreign affairs for his few significant accomplishments. During his administration, Alaska was purchased from Russia, but at that time many Americans scorned the acquisition because they did not recognize the potential wealth and strategic location of this northern wilderness.

In 1867 Johnson achieved another diplomatic success, this time in the country that shares the southern boundary of the United States. During the Civil War, Napoleon III of France had sent troops to Mexico and installed Austrian Archduke Maximilian on the Mexican throne. Asserting that France had violated the Monroe Doctrine, Johnson declared that the French soldiers must be withdrawn. To strengthen his demand, he sent 50,000 soldiers to the Mexican border. Napoleon III then backed down, called the French forces home from Mexico, and allowed the helpless Maximilian to be captured and executed by Mexican insurgents.

As Johnson's presidential term drew near its end, the Republicans were anxious to cast aside the man they had eagerly elected vice president four years earlier. But Johnson refused to relinquish his political ambitions. Returning to the Democratic party, he sought in vain its 1868 presidential nomination. The next year he tried unsuccessfully to win back his Senate seat in Tennessee, and in 1872 he made a futile bid to be elected to the House of Representatives. But the stubborn warrior from Greeneville persisted, and in 1874 he became the first and only former president to be elected to the Senate. When Johnson took back the Tennessee Senate seat that he had relinquished twelve years before in order to become military governor of his war-torn state, there were bouquets of flowers on his desk and warm greetings from old colleagues, including some who had voted against him in his impeachment trial.

The former president served only a few months of his Senate term. He suffered a stroke and died on July 31, 1875. Johnson was buried in Greeneville, his body wrapped in an American flag and his head resting on a copy of the Constitution. The simple but appropriate message on his tombstone read: "His faith in the people never wavered."

It is difficult to evaluate Andrew Johnson's record as president. His impeachment trial and the closeness of the vote to unseat him cast a long, dark shadow over his administration. Obviously Johnson was naive in closing his eyes to the return of white supremacy in the postwar South, and he failed to understand that the federal government had a responsibility to respond to the economic and political needs of the former slaves. Moreover, other presidents have not always maintained amicable relations with Congress, but few of them stooped to Johnson's level and directed crude, personal insults at their political opponents.

On the other hand, Johnson was a man of remarkable courage, dogged determination, and endless perseverance. And to his credit was his genuine concern for the common, ordinary people, which sprang from a lifelong conviction that the American Dream must be shared with the underprivileged.

Johnson's reputation has suffered when he has been compared with the much loved, martyred Lincoln, in whose footsteps he had to follow. But since the Reconstruction programs of both presidents were quite similar, historians have long wondered how Lincoln, had he not been assassinated, would have fared in the difficult task of restoring a fragmented Union. Undoubtedly he would have demonstrated more tact and a greater talent for conciliation and compromise than Johnson possessed. But the central question still remains: Would Lincoln have avoided the pitfalls that brought Johnson's presidency to the brink of disaster? No one knows the answer.

Chapter 5
Chester Alan Arthur:
From Spoilsman to
Reformer

Controversy surrounded both the date and the place of birth of the twenty-first president. Chester Alan Arthur was born October 5, 1829, but in middle age— trying to make himself seem younger—Arthur began telling people falsely that he had been born in 1830. His duplicity was widely accepted, and most nineteenth-century accounts of his life gave the wrong year for his birth.

Chester probably was born in the village of Fairfield, Vermont, but some family friends contended that his birth took place at nearby Waterville. And when he was a candidate for vice president, political opponents claimed that he was born in Canada, a short distance across the Vermont border. Had this been true, Arthur would have been constitutionally disqualified from becoming either vice president or president. But no evidence was uncovered to prove that he was not born in the United States.

One explanation for the confusion about the site of the future president's birth was that his family moved frequently during his childhood. Chester's father, William, was an Irish immigrant who became a Baptist preacher after teaching a few years in New England. Although an eloquent speaker, Reverend Arthur had a disagreeable, scolding manner that often made him unpopular with congregations. So, along with his wife and nine children, he transferred from parish to parish in Vermont and New York.

During the first nine years of his life, Chester moved with his family five times, settling at last in Union Village (now Greenwich), New York, where he attended the local academy. Five years later the Arthurs moved to Schenectady. There, chiefly because his father had taught him Latin and Greek, Chester was admitted to Union College as a sophomore at the age of fifteen. He helped to pay his way through college by teaching school, and he graduated at eighteen in the top third of his class.

The tall, handsome young man decided to become a lawyer, but his family could offer no financial assistance, so Arthur continued teaching while studying law. In 1853 he moved to New York City, and the following year he was admitted to the bar.

Arthur was an abolitionist, and as a young attorney he helped argue two cases involving the rights of blacks. In one case, Jonathan Lemmon had brought eight slaves from Virginia to New York City by boat. The group intended to stop over only until the next boat left for Texas. But when the slaves' presence was discovered, a free black man obtained a court order declaring they were free, since a state law permitted no person to be held in bondage. Lemmon refused to accept this decision. His attorneys argued in court that the slaves were merely passing through New York, were not residents of the state, and that their ownership could not be disputed because of their travel. The case eventually reached the New York

State Court of Appeals, which agreed with Arthur's position that Lemmon's slaves were entitled to freedom.

In the other discrimination case, Arthur was the attorney for a black woman who had been forced off a Brooklyn streetcar because she refused to leave a section reserved for whites. Arthur won $250 in damages for his client. More important, the court decreed that on all of New York State's public transportation facilities blacks must be allowed the same accommodations as white passengers.

To expand his legal practice, Arthur needed to enlarge his circle of acquaintances, so he joined social clubs and entered politics. He had a genial manner and delighted listeners with entertaining stories based on a remarkable fund of knowledge. Soon his group of friends included prominent politicians, literary figures, and business leaders. With his political friends, Arthur helped organize the new Republican party in the state of New York, but he showed no interest in running for office.

In 1856 Arthur was introduced to Ellen (Nell) Herndon from Virginia, the nineteen-year-old daughter of a naval officer. They began dating and soon became engaged, but their courtship was interrupted when Arthur traveled west on a long visit to the Kansas Territory. Rumor had it that large fortunes could be made in the region, and Arthur considered buying land there and perhaps settling with Nell in a frontier town.

Arthur was called home by news of the death of his fiancée's father, Captain William Herndon. When Arthur returned to New York to be with Nell and her family, he gave up the idea of moving to Kansas. In 1859 he and Nell were married in New York City's Calvary Episcopalian Church. The couple had three children, two sons and a daughter. The older son,

William, died before he was three years old; partly because of his death, the Arthurs pampered and spoiled their younger son, Chester Alan II.

When the Civil War started in 1861, Nell and Chester found themselves on opposite sides. With her Virginian background and relatives fighting in the Confederate forces, Nell privately was sympathetic to the South. Abolitionist Chester, on the other hand, had served in the New York State militia since 1858, and when hostilities broke out he strongly supported the Union cause.

The day after the war began Arthur was assigned the important military position of assistant quartermaster general, with the rank of brigadier general. It was his job to devise methods for feeding, housing, and equipping the thousands of war-bound soldiers flooding into New York City from all over the Northeast. Wading through mountains of paper work, he set about ordering military uniforms and supplies, finding food for the troops, and supervising the building of temporary barracks. Arthur won praise as a capable, effective administrator, and in 1862 he was promoted to the position of quartermaster general for the entire state of New York.

After the war Arthur divided his time between his successful law practice and an increasingly active role in New York State politics. He identified with the most conservative faction of the Republican party, called the Stalwarts. The leader of the Stalwarts in New York was flamboyant, powerful Senator Roscoe Conkling, and Arthur became Conkling's chief lieutenant. Together they worked hard for the election of Ulysses S. Grant as president in 1868.

During the Gilded Age that followed the Civil War, the spoils system, much more than issues, dominated American politics. The spoils system (derived from the term "to the victor belongs the spoils") called for victorious candidates to award government jobs to political supporters and friends. In return, these government workers were expected to pay a percentage of their salaries into the party treasury and perform party duties. President Grant, relying on the advice of political bosses like Conkling, gave thousands of government positions to his loyal campaigners. In 1871 he rewarded Arthur by appointing him to one of the most lucrative posts, collector of customs for the port of New York.

The New York Customhouse was of vital importance to the nation's economy in the late 1800s. About three-fourths of all tariff revenue, amounting to more than $100 million a year, was collected there. When Arthur became its collector, it was estimated that this customhouse did an annual business five times greater than that of the largest business house in North America.[1]

The customhouse employed about 1,000 people, and Arthur maintained tightfisted control over all the workers. When vacancies occurred, he filled them with faithful party supporters, and he ordered employees to make "voluntary contributions" to the party coffers. Although charges of corruption were leveled at the operation of the customhouse, Arthur did not use his job for dishonest personal profit. He and his family lived comfortably on the income derived legitimately from his position, about $50,000 a year; the collector of customs was paid as much as the president of the United States and five times more than the vice president or Supreme Court justices!

In 1872 Arthur supported Grant for a second term, raising contributions for the president's campaign from customhouse workers and other sources throughout the state of New York. He proved to be one of the Republicans' most successful fund-raisers and an able organizer of the party machine. Always an elegant dresser with impeccable manners, Arthur acquired the nickname "Gentleman Boss."

After Grant's two terms in the White House, Arthur campaigned for the presidential nomination of his own boss, Roscoe Conkling, in 1876. But the Republican party, damaged by widespread graft and corruption in the Grant administration, wanted to steer clear of a Stalwart machine politician like Conkling and gave its nomination instead to Rutherford B. Hayes, the reform-minded governor of Ohio. Hayes barely defeated his Democratic opponent, Governor Samuel J. Tilden of New York, in the hotly disputed presidential election.

Once elected, President Hayes appointed a commission to investigate the charges of corruption in the New York Customhouse. Arthur was the first witness, and he gave six hours of testimony but was unable to convince his interrogators that his agency was being run properly and efficiently. The commission concluded that Arthur had padded the customhouse payroll with too many employees, nearly all of them hired for their party loyalty rather than their ability to perform their jobs competently. And the commission was highly critical of Arthur's policy to force civil servants to kick back part of their salaries to a political party.

President Hayes agreed with the commission's recommendation that the New York Customhouse reduce its work force and be reorganized on a strictly nonpartisan basis. He issued an order forbidding its employees to engage actively in partisan politics or make forced contributions to party treasuries. When Arthur refused to comply with these demands, Hayes tried to ease him out of office by offering him a diplomatic post in Paris. The "Gentleman Boss" turned this down, and Hayes dismissed him as collector of customs in July 1878.

Losing his high-paying government job did not deter Arthur from continuing his favorite activity, politicking. He traveled extensively throughout New York, helping many Stalwart candidates in their election campaigns. And night after night he sat up until two or three in the morning talking politics, eating, drinking, and smoking cigars with his political cronies. Often, a few hours before dawn, he would coax a friend to continue their political discussion while they walked several blocks through the darkened neighborhood.

Arthur was so busy with his political pursuits and law practice that he spent little time with his wife and children. Nell probably resented her husband's frequent absences, but she never criticized him publicly for neglecting her. Most of her time was spent caring for their children and managing their large New York City house. She also took a keen interest in musical events. Nell was a talented soprano, and in her younger years she sang with the Mendelssohn Glee Club and at benefit performances. Later she attended concerts and operas with relatives.

One evening in January 1880, Nell caught cold while waiting outside for a carriage following a concert. She developed pneumonia, and her condition deteriorated quickly. Arthur, in Albany on a political errand, was summoned home. By the time he reached her bedside, Nell was unconscious, and she died the next day.

Arthur was overwhelmed emotionally by the death of his forty-two-year-old wife. For weeks he was desolate, unable to overcome his grief or shake off his guilty feelings for long neglecting his wife. The door to Ellen's bedroom was closed, and her husband ordered that her room never be touched again.[2]

The 1880 presidential election revived Arthur's

spirits, and he plunged into the campaign with enthusiasm and determination. The Stalwarts' candidate was former President Ulysses S. Grant, who wanted to return to the White House, even though his two-term administration had been severely marred by officeholders engaged in graft and corruption. Largely because of his military leadership in the Civil War, Grant was still a popular hero with many Americans. Others, however, were reluctant to award a third term to a president whose previous terms had produced a shameful record. At the Republican convention the anti-Grant delegates supported Senator James G. Blaine of Maine, Treasury Secretary John Sherman of Ohio, and some favorite sons.

Grant jumped into the lead on the first ballot for the presidential nomination, with 304 votes, 65 short of the number needed for a majority. Blaine was a close second with 279 votes, and Sherman had only 91. Ballot after ballot, the anti-Grant forces prevented the Civil War general from getting the nomination. But they needed an alternate candidate who would achieve a majority, and they could not agree on the alternate. Finally, on the thirty-sixth ballot, they selected a compromise choice, James A. Garfield, an Ohio congressman who had been a northern major general in the Civil War, and Garfield won the nomination. Ironically, Garfield had come to the convention as Sherman's campaign manager and had given the nominating speech for his fellow Ohioan.

The Stalwarts were so angry and disappointed that Grant had not been given the nomination that some of them threatened not to work for Garfield in the fall election. So the Republican chieftains, anxious to unite their warring factions, decided that the second place on the ticket should be given to a Stalwart from New York, which was the most populous state and had the most electoral votes. They first asked

Levi P. Morton, a prominent New York banker, to be Garfield's running mate. He turned them down, and the convention leaders then approached Arthur. The former collector of customs gratefully accepted the offer to run with Garfield, declaring, "The office of the Vice-President is a greater honor than I ever dreamed of attaining."[3] On the first ballot, Arthur easily won the nomination.

Many Republicans and most Democrats were outraged that Arthur would be a candidate for the second-highest office in the land. John Sherman bitterly described the selection of Arthur as a "ridiculous burlesque" and concluded that "the only reason for his nomination was that he was discharged from an office that he was unfit to fill." The *Louisville Courier-Journal* ran a picture of Arthur with the caption "Nominated at Chicago for the Vice-Presidency. Suspended by President Hayes from the New York Collectorship, that the office might be honestly administered."[4]

E. L. Godkin, the editor of *Nation*, looking at Arthur's nomination from a different perspective, observed that ". . . there is no place in which [Arthur's] powers of mischief will be so small as in the Vice-Presidency." Then he added, "It is true General Garfield, if elected, may die during his term of office, but this is too unlikely a contingency to be worth making extraordinary provisions for."[5]

The Democrats also named a Civil War general, Winfield Scott Hancock of Pennsylvania, as their standard-bearer. They felt confident about their chances to recapture the White House for the first time since the election of 1856. Tilden had lost by a whisker in 1876, when a few southern states, still occupied by northern carpetbaggers, voted Republican; now, in 1880, all of the southern states were back under Democratic control.

Arthur played a major role in this hard-fought campaign. As chairman of the New York State Republican Committee, he organized scores of meetings and rallies. He took personal charge of campaign visits by Grant and Conkling into the doubtful states of Ohio and Indiana, and he coaxed contributions from New York businessmen to a secret fund to be used in Indiana. Also, he assessed many officeholders 3 percent of their salaries as "voluntary contributions" to the party treasury.[6]

The results of the 1880 election were unusual: Garfield and Arthur won an impressive victory in the electoral vote, but their edge in the popular vote was only razor thin. The Republican ticket carried nearly the entire North and West, amassing 214 electoral votes to the Democrats' 155. But Garfield's popular-vote margin was less than 2,000 out of more than 9 million votes cast; the 1880 contest provided the closest popular vote of any presidential election in American history.

As soon as Garfield had taken the oath of office, he was confronted by long lines of politicians asking for jobs in the new administration. Much of his time had to be spent listening to their pleas and trying to find offices for those who seemed competent or wielded the most influence. Disgusted and weary from this unpleasant experience, at one point Garfield exclaimed, "My God! What is there in this place that a man should ever want to get into it?"[7] The new president told his associates that some kind of civil service reforms must be established to replace the scandalous spoils system.

Garfield, however, had little time to bring about changes in the way government job applications were handled. On July 2, 1881, less than four months after he took office, the president was shot in the back by Charles Guiteau, a mentally unbalanced office seeker.

When the police seized him, the deranged assassin screamed defiantly, "I am a Stalwart, and Arthur will be president."[8] While held in custody, Guiteau claimed he had sought revenge against Garfield for not granting his request for a diplomatic post in either Vienna or Paris, and he implied that Arthur, if president, would have given him the job he wanted. Guiteau was later found guilty of murder and executed.

Garfield lingered in failing health for more than two months, and during this period there was enormous criticism of the vice president. To many Americans, Arthur was the supreme example of the corrupt political boss, a hated symbol of all that was wrong with the spoils system. There even were false but cruel accusations that Guiteau had been a hired killer employed by the Stalwarts to get rid of the president. A host of newspapers questioned Arthur's fitness to serve as chief executive. The *New York Times* bluntly declared:

> *Active politicians, uncompromising partisans, have held before now the office of Vice-President of the United States, but no holder of that office has ever made it so plainly subordinate to his self-interest as a politician and his narrowness as a partisan. . . . While his succession to the Presidency of the United States depends simply on the issue of a strong man's struggle with death, Gen. Arthur is about the last man who would be considered eligible to that position, did the choice depend on the voice either of a majority of his own party or of a majority of the people of the United States.*[9]

Friends who saw Arthur as he solemnly awaited the call to assume the presidency said he appeared despondent and tense. He had never coveted the highest office in the government, and he was acutely sensitive to the bitter attacks waged against him in the nation's press. When Arthur learned that Garfield had died on September 19, he received the news with childlike sobs. The following day the presidential oath was administered to him at his New York home. The oath was repeated two days later in the vice president's Capitol office, with former presidents Grant and Hayes present for the brief ceremony.

The movement for civil service reform had begun in the Grant administration, but it took on new urgency after the assassination of Garfield. From all parts of the nation, voices were raised to do away with the spoils system and eyes were riveted on the new chief executive to see what stand he would take on this important issue.

President Arthur pledged his full cooperation to help provide a new civil service system for federal employees, and Congress responded to the national outcry for this significant reform. Senator George Pendleton of Ohio introduced a bill calling for sweeping changes, including the creation of a bipartisan three-member commission to devise civil service rules. Other provisions included competitive examinations for positions on a list of classified jobs, a period of probation required to test a jobholder's fitness, promotion based only on merit and competence, and the abolition of compulsory financial assessments on officeholders.

When the Pendleton bill (1883) passed in Congress and reached President Arthur's desk, the man who had been called "Gentleman Boss" signed it into law. And the president was widely praised for appointing to the first civil service commission outstanding men whose performance was free of partisan bias. (At first the list of offices covered by civil service was limited to about 10,000 positions, but subsequent presidents greatly enlarged the list.)

One issue that plagued the Arthur administration has not troubled twentieth-century presidents. In 1881 there was a huge surplus of money in the Treasury, caused mainly by high tariffs and low government expenditures. This created a problem because with each increase in Treasury funds, more money was taken out of circulation, causing a deflation of prices. President Arthur asked Congress for a reduction in tariff rates and appointed a commission to investigate ways in which these rates could be cut. The commission worked hard for several months, hearing hundreds of witnesses and compiling nearly 3,000 pages of testimony. In its final report, the commission called for a substantial reduction in duties.

Many powerful manufacturers, however, exerted strong influence on Congress and the president to keep high, protectionist rates. As a result, the so-called "Mongrel Tariff" of 1883 reduced duties on the average of only 1.47 percent. For many years afterward the tariff continued to be one of the political parties' most hotly debated issues: Republicans generally favored higher tariffs, while most Democrats supported lower rates.

Another problem that faced the nation during Arthur's presidency was what to do about Chinese immigration and citizenship. During the 1850s and 1860s, Americans had welcomed Chinese laborers to help construct railroads and work in the gold mines in the West. But once the railroads were completed and the Gold Rush ended, the public attitude toward Chinese immigration changed drastically, especially in the West, where most Chinese had settled. Opposition centered around the foreigners' customs, which were attacked as "anti-Christian," their alleged vice and filth, and, most important, their willingness to work for much lower wages than white people would accept.

In 1882 Senator John Miller of California introduced a bill that would have excluded Chinese laborers for twenty years and denied citizenship to Chinese residents. After the bill passed both houses of Congress, President Arthur vetoed it. He declared that suspending Chinese immigration for as long as twenty years was an unreasonable requirement, and he objected to the provision preventing the Chinese from obtaining citizenship.

Congressional leaders then revised the bill, reducing the exclusion of Chinese immigration to ten years. The president signed this bill, although he was reluctant to do so because it still denied American citizenship to Chinese residents. (This provision was renewed in 1892 and 1902 and not repealed until 1943, when China and the United States were allies in World War II.)

President Arthur and Congress crossed swords again when a bill was passed appropriating $19 million for the improvement of rivers and harbors. Arthur vetoed this bill because he felt it was "pork barrel" legislation that provided a large sum of federal money on local projects not critically needed. The president lost this battle when Congress overrode his veto.

One of Arthur's chief achievements dealt with the need for a better navy. At the time that he became president, the United States Navy was inferior to those of all the major European nations and several Latin American countries. Other nations were then constructing steel ships. The American vessels, mostly built for the Civil War and badly in need of repair, were all made of wood, except for four of the

88

smallest ships, which had iron hulls. Arthur skillfully won from Congress appropriations for four new steel ships—three cruisers and a dispatch vessel. This called for a modest investment, but it marked the beginning of the United States' modern navy.

In various proposals that President Arthur made to Congress, he seemed to be ahead of his time. He asked Congress to consider the matter of presidential succession and determine when a vice president becomes an acting president, so as to avoid the kind of situation that developed when Garfield lay mortally wounded for many weeks. (This was finally resolved by the Twenty-fifth Amendment, adopted in 1967.) Mindful of rate abuses and other unfair practices of railroad companies, Arthur spoke out in favor of the regulation of interstate commerce. (Congress passed the Interstate Commerce Act two years after he left office.) Arthur also sought an item veto, whereby a president could block certain portions of a bill while accepting others. (Presidents still do not have the item veto, but this idea has been strongly endorsed by recent chief executives, including Ronald Reagan and George Bush.)

After Arthur became president he seldom was called "Gentleman Boss." Instead, the press described him as "Elegant Arthur" and the "Dude President." Although he had grown heavy by middle age, the 6-foot 2-inch president had a commanding appearance. His posture was erect, his gait was confident, his wavy dark hair was carefully combed, and his gray side whiskers were neatly trimmed.

Arthur spent much time and money selecting what he considered proper clothes for a president to wear. (It was rumored that he owned eighty pairs of pants and would try on twenty new pairs before deciding which ones to add to his large collection.) He wore fashionable tweeds in the morning, black frock coats with white or gray waistcoats and gray trousers in the afternoon, and a tuxedo at dinner.

Before moving into the White House, Arthur had the famous building redecorated, supervising the project himself. Twenty-four wagonloads of historic furniture and household items dating back to the first Adams administration were taken from the premises and sold at public auction. New furniture was purchased, walls were painted or adorned with beautiful wallpaper, exquisite carpets were laid on floors, handsome draperies were hung at the windows.

The president hosted many elegant state dinners and other parties, with his youngest sister, Mary McElroy, acting as hostess. He thoroughly enjoyed good company, excellent food and liquor, and expensive cigars. Sometimes his dinners would include fourteen courses and eight kinds of wine; guests would spend two to three hours in the dining room, eating, drinking, and engaging in lively conversation.

All was not serene, however, for the genial host. Arthur sorely missed his wife, who had died less than two years before he became president. He ordered a fresh bouquet of flowers placed daily before her portrait in the White House. And his lavish, frequent entertaining, according to close friends, was partly inspired by the need to compensate for his loneliness.

While he was president, Arthur learned that he had Bright's disease, a serious kidney ailment that was then almost always fatal. This disease caused him to suffer nausea, depression, weakness, and extreme weariness. But Arthur was determined to keep his illness a secret, and he denied newspaper accounts suggesting that he was sick.

When his term of office was nearing its end, Arthur made a halfhearted bid for another term. He knew that ill health almost certainly would have prevented him from serving four more years, and he was convinced that the Republican party would turn to James G. Blaine to head its ticket in 1884. But Arthur did not want to be considered a quitter, so he let his name be placed in nomination for the presidency. Even though he did not wage an active campaign, on the first ballot at the Republican convention the president received 278 delegate votes out of a total of 820 votes cast. Blaine, as expected, was nominated on the fourth ballot, but he lost the close presidential race to Democrat Grover Cleveland.

After he left the White House, Arthur resumed practicing law, but his declining health prevented him from doing much work. He suffered a stroke on November 17, 1886, and died the next day. The former president was buried next to his wife in Albany, New York.

No vice president who succeeded to the presidency ever took over the reins of government under the cloud of suspicion and criticism that enveloped Arthur when he entered the White House. The public feared that the "Gentleman Boss" who never had been elected to any office before he became vice president would have a disastrous administration. Legitimate questions were raised about whether the new president would perform his duties efficiently and honestly, and avoid manipulation by greedy, power-seeking machine politicians. Arthur, however, surprised his critics by establishing a competent administration that was free of the charges of graft and corruption that had plagued the previous Stalwart president, Ulysses S. Grant.

Arthur's presidency did not provide many outstanding achievements, but it must be remembered that he served at a time when the chief executive was clearly subordinate to Congress. None of the other presidents who served in the last third of the nineteenth century was able to leave a strong record as the nation's chief policy-maker. Arthur, at least, was willing to stand up to Congress, as demonstrated by his opposition to the first Chinese exclusion bill and the rivers and harbors bill. And he earned the respect of a grateful public by reversing his role as a spoilsman to champion the cause of civil service rights.

Chapter 6
Theodore Roosevelt:
The Robust President

Theodore Roosevelt, who was born in New York City on October 27, 1858, came from a wealthy, socially prominent family. In the nineteenth century most people of his social class frowned on political careers, considering them degrading and beneath their dignity. Yet politics became Roosevelt's consuming passion, and, even more ironic, this son of a rich businessman became a progressive reformer intent on using the government to regulate big business, broaden control of the railroads, attack serious social problems, and conserve natural resources.

Roosevelt's father, Theodore, Sr., was a prosperous importer and also was active in banking. The Roosevelt family lived in a luxurious home in a fashionable part of the city. "Teddy" had an older sister, Anna, a younger brother, Elliott (father of Eleanor Roosevelt), and a younger sister, Corinne.

Teddy suffered from severe asthma almost from birth, and often at night he sat propped up in bed by pillows, gasping for breath. Some evenings his father bundled Teddy in blankets and took him for a walk or a carriage ride through dark, deserted streets, hoping that the night breeze would give the child relief. Beginning in childhood, Teddy also was handicapped by extreme nearsightedness, and he had to wear glasses with very thick lenses.

When Teddy was eleven, his father had a small gymnasium built for him in their home, and the young boy began lifting weights and swinging on parallel bars. But two years later he had a humiliating experience at a summer camp. Two of the other boys took advantage of the puny, nearsighted camper by shoving and punching him. Unable to fight back, Teddy felt so frustrated that he resolved to learn to defend himself.

Teddy began taking boxing lessons from a former prizefighter. He was a painfully slow and awkward pupil, and he admitted that he boxed two or three years before there was any noticeable improvement. Then one day he won a pewter mug in a class tournament. This inexpensive mug represented Teddy's first victory over his physical weakness, and for the rest of his life it was one of his most prized possessions.[1]

Young Roosevelt showed a keen interest in natural history, and had he not entered politics, he probably would have become a professional naturalist. At age seven, he observed a dead seal at a fish market. With a folding pocket ruler, he measured the seal and recorded the figures in a notebook. "That seal," he later recalled, "filled me with every possible feeling of romance and adventure."[2] Somehow he acquired the seal's head and, with the help of two cousins, started what he called the "Roosevelt Museum of Natural History." Teddy later snared mice, birds, frogs, spiders, crickets, and other insects, which

94

he killed, catalogued, and stored in a dresser on an upstairs porch at the rear of his house.

Teddy never went to public school. For a while his Aunt Anna taught him, and later he had a succession of tutors. He spent the summer of 1873 in Dresden, Germany, studying German and French. Impressed by Roosevelt's keen mind and extraordinary memory, his teacher predicted, "He will surely one day be a great professor, or who knows, he may become president of the United States."[3]

In 1876 Teddy entered Harvard, where, he said confidently, his aim was to become a successful naturalist like John James Audubon. He was a serious scholar, graduating Phi Beta Kappa and magna cum laude, twenty-first of 177 students in the class of 1880. Teddy still found time for many extracurricular activities. He joined various campus clubs and in his senior year started writing *The Naval War of 1812*, which, when published in 1882, was hailed as a classic in its field. (During his lifetime, Roosevelt wrote twenty-one books—far more than any other president.)

While at Harvard Teddy continued boxing, and by this time he could hold his own in the ring with the best college boxers. As a junior he entered the competition for Harvard's lightweight boxing championship and advanced to the final round. He lost that bout to a senior, who later admitted that Roosevelt was "far more scientific" and, "given good eyes, he would have defeated me easily."[4]

In the same year that Roosevelt graduated from college, he married Alice Lee, the beautiful daughter of a prominent Boston banker. They went to live in New York City with Teddy's mother, now widowed. Roosevelt enrolled at Columbia Law School, but he found his law classes tedious and boring. He sought diversion by joining the National Guard, riding horseback through Central Park and in polo matches, taking marathon walks, and, while on vacation, climbing the Matterhorn in Switzerland.

Craving more action, the restless young man joined a Republican club and turned his attention to a political career. He dropped out of law school and ran for a seat in the New York State Assembly. This horrified some of his upper-class friends, who declared that politics was a dirty business run by society's most disreputable elements. Roosevelt bluntly replied:

> . . . If this were so, it merely meant that the people I knew did not belong to the governing class and that the other people did—and that I intended to be one of the governing class; . . . I certainly would not quit until I . . . found out that I really was too weak to hold my own in the rough and tumble.[5]

Roosevelt won the election and, at the age of twenty-three, was the youngest member of the Assembly. He was twice reelected to this office. Never timid or reluctant to speak out against what he felt was wrong, the young assemblyman accused financier Jay Gould of trying to corrupt a New York State supreme court justice. He charged that Gould belonged to the most dangerous of classes, the wealthy criminal class. Experienced legislators were flabbergasted to hear a young upstart dare to attack an influential man like Gould, but Roosevelt was serving notice that no one, no matter how powerful, could intimidate him.

Tragedy struck the young assemblyman in February 1884. While the legislature was in session at Albany, Roosevelt received word that his wife had given birth to a baby girl. Before he had time to catch a train home, a second telegram arrived, saying that

96

*"AND WHEN YOU PRESS THIS BUTTON
HERE HE SINGS 'GOD BLESS AMERICA'
AND 'YANKEE DOODLE DANDY.' "*

*The presidential campaign of 1840 was characterized
by many parades such as this one.*

John Tyler, who succeeded to the presidency after the death of William Henry Harrison in 1841, became the first "accidental" president.

A Whig campaign banner of the 1848 presidential convention

Above: Ad that appeared in a Raleigh, North Carolina, newspaper when Andrew Johnson, then a tailor's apprentice, ran away

Right: Before the 1866 congressional elections, President Andrew Johnson embarked on a long tour around the country, imploring the citizens not to elect more Radical Republicans to Congress. The trip was not a success— the election produced even more Radical Republicans in Congress.

Above: Chester Alan Arthur takes the presidential oath of office at his New York residence.

Left: The only president of the United States to be tried for impeachment, here Johnson accepts the summons presented by the sergeant-at-arms of the Senate.

*Theodore Roosevelt and naturalist John Muir at
Yosemite Park. Roosevelt was a bold environ-
mentalist at a time when little interest was shown
in protecting the environment and our natural
resources for future generations.*

*President Roosevelt delivering an
emotionally charged speech*

Calvin Coolidge sworn in as president of the United States by his father, a justice of the peace, at his father's home in Plymouth Notch, Vermont, on August 3, 1923

*Coolidge trout fishing after his presidency ended; he
nearly always wore a suit and hat when he fished.*

Far left: World War I saw Harry S Truman serving in the Army in Europe.

Left: Truman is sworn in as president after Franklin Roosevelt died on April 12, 1945. At his side are his wife, Bess, and his daughter, Margaret.

Below: President Truman is cheered as he rides along 125th Street in New York City's Harlem section during his campaign tour of the city in October 1948.

Far left: World War I saw Harry S Truman serving in the Army in Europe.

Left: Truman is sworn in as president after Franklin Roosevelt died on April 12, 1945. At his side are his wife, Bess, and his daughter, Margaret.

Below: President Truman is cheered as he rides along 125th Street in New York City's Harlem section during his campaign tour of the city in October 1948.

Left: Lyndon Baines Johnson being administered the presidential oath by federal judge Sarah T. Hughes aboard Air Force One *after President John F. Kennedy was assassinated on November 22, 1963. He is flanked by Mrs. Johnson, left, and Mrs. Kennedy.*

Below: President Johnson signed a large number of bills during his presidency that were designed to help bring about the "Great Society."

*Gerald R. Ford takes the oath of office as the
thirty-eighth president of the United States. Chief
Justice Warren Burger administers the oath.*

his wife was gravely ill. When his horse-driven cab drew up to the family house, his brother Elliott greeted him with the sad message that Alice was dying from Bright's disease and childbirth complications, and their mother was dying from typhoid fever. The two most important women in Teddy's life passed away on the same day, February 14, the fourth anniversary of his engagement to Alice. (The baby, also named Alice, survived. By the time she was a teenager, Alice was well known for her unconventional behavior and sarcastic wit. She married Ohio Congressman Nicholas Longworth, who later became speaker of the House. "Princess Alice," as the press called her, entertained many presidents in her Washington home and was one of the capital's most famous residents until her death at age ninety-six in 1980.)

Roosevelt was overwhelmed with grief, but he felt it was his duty to return to the job that the people of his district had elected him to hold. As soon as the legislature's session ended, he announced that he would not stand for reelection. Instead, he left his infant daughter with his sister Anna and headed west to the Dakota Badlands.

For the next two years he threw himself into the rough life of the frontier, rounding up cattle and breaking stampedes, riding countless miles in search of buffalo and other animals, and, while hunting, sleeping outdoors on a blanket, even when it rained. He earned the respect of the rugged cowboys, who at first had looked upon the dude from New York with his pince-nez glasses as a "four-eyed tenderfoot." Roosevelt's experiences in the West renewed his vigor and gave him the strength and confidence needed to put behind him the tragedies he had endured.

Returning to the East, Roosevelt plunged back

into politics, running for mayor of New York City in 1886. He finished third in the race and spent most of the next three years writing history books.

Roosevelt's mood sharpened brightly when, in December 1886, he married Edith Kermit Carow, a childhood playmate who had lived next door. They became the parents of five children, four sons and one daughter.

In 1888 Roosevelt campaigned for the election of Republican Benjamin Harrison to the presidency. After Harrison won the election, he appointed the former New York assemblyman to the position of civil service commissioner. This government office seldom attracted much publicity, but Roosevelt captured headlines by working exhaustively for civil service reform. Much to the displeasure of many political appointees who were forced to resign, the number of jobs placed on the civil service list more than doubled during the six years that Roosevelt was a commissioner.

Even more attention was focused on Roosevelt, whom newspapers began referring to as T.R., when he became president of New York City's Board of Police Commissioners in 1895. T.R. fought persistently against corruption and laziness in the police force. To make sure that the police were performing their duties, he sometimes prowled the streets from midnight to dawn, partially disguised in a black cloak and a wide-brimmed hat pulled down over much of his face. He strictly enforced a law banning the sale of liquor on Sunday, shutting down offending bars in the city and fining their owners.

After William McKinley assumed the presidency in 1897, he named Roosevelt assistant secretary of the Navy. The energetic zeal with which T.R. pursued his new job exasperated ailing, slow-moving Navy

Secretary John D. Long, who described Roosevelt in this way:

He is full of suggestions, many of which are of great value, and his spirit and forceful habit is a good tonic; but the very devil seems to possess him— distributing ships, ordering ammunition which there is no means to move to places where there is no means to store it; sending messages to Congress for immediate legislation authorizing the enlistment of an unlimited number of seamen.[6]

When the battleship U.S.S. *Maine* exploded and sank in Havana harbor on February 15, 1898, Roosevelt jumped to the conclusion that this act of treachery was committed by the Spaniards, who then owned Cuba. He fervently believed that the United States should go to war with Spain to free Cuba. Ten days later, when Secretary Long was not in his office, Roosevelt cabled Commodore George Dewey, commander of the American Asiatic Squadron, boldly ordering him to be ready to attack the Spanish fleet in the Philippines should war break out. Although the assistant secretary of the navy lacked the authority to issue such an order without the approval of his superiors, he justified his action on the ground that it was a prudent step to take.

When the war started, Roosevelt resigned from his office job so that he could take part in the fighting. Commissioned a lieutenant colonel, he helped form a volunteer cavalry regiment and requested the enlistment of cowboys he knew in the West and polo-playing friends in the East. Because of its many expert equestrians, the regiment came to be known as the "Rough Riders." However, most of the famous "Rough Riders" saw no military action astride their horses. When their regiment sailed from Tampa, Florida, to the Cuban coast, the transport ships were so crowded that the only horses aboard were those that belonged to the officers. So most of the cavalrymen who followed Roosevelt in the charge on Kettle Hill (often wrongly called the charge on San Juan Hill) did so on foot. Nevertheless, the campaign against the Spanish troops in Cuba was highly successful, and T.R. emerged from the war a national hero.

The Republican boss in New York, Senator Thomas C. Platt, knew that his party needed a powerful candidate for governor in the 1898 election. When Roosevelt's name was mentioned, Platt had some reservations because he knew that T.R. favored reform measures that he, Platt, opposed. But the Spanish-American War hero was the most popular Republican in the state and probably the only man who stood a chance to defeat the strong Democratic candidate for governor, Judge Augustus van Wyck. So Platt reluctantly consented to the nomination of Roosevelt, who then made an energetic railroad tour of the state. The election was close; T.R. won by a slim margin of 18,000 votes out of more than 1,200,000 votes cast.

Governor Roosevelt lost no time in pushing bills he wanted through the New York legislature. He obtained laws to curb sweatshop abuses, supervise utilities and insurance companies, limit the number of hours that women and children could work, reform the handling of food and drugs, and tighten civil service requirements. The Roosevelt-sponsored measure that drew the most attention called for state taxation of corporations. Senator Platt, the chief spokesman of big business in New York, fought against this bill and managed for a while to keep the legislature from acting on it. But the governor ral-

lied such a huge public outcry for taxing corporations that the bill finally passed.

When Boss Platt discovered, much to his disap-
pointment, that he could not control Roosevelt, he
set out to prevent the governor's reelection. Vice
President Garret Hobart had died in 1899, and Platt
began promoting Roosevelt for the second spot on
the Republican ticket in 1900, as a way of getting the
reforming "Rough Rider" out of New York politics.
Platt was very pleased that President William Mc-
Kinley refused to express a preference for a vice
presidential running mate. But Ohio Senator Mark
Hanna, who was also the Republican party national
chairman, was horrified when he learned that the
movement to nominate Roosevelt was gaining strength
at the convention. "Don't any of you realize," he cried
out angrily to other Republican leaders, "that there's
only one life between that madman and the Presidency?"[7]

At first T.R. was reluctant to run for the vice
presidency, figuring that in this almost powerless position he could accomplish little. But the egotistical
governor of New York wanted to prove that he could
win the nomination, and he listened to friends who
said that this office might be his springboard to the
presidency. So Roosevelt finally consented to accept
second place on the ticket.

McKinley's Democratic opponent was the fiery
orator William Jennings Bryan, the same candidate
for the presidency he had defeated four years before. As in 1896, McKinley again did not conduct a
strenuous campaign. Most of the stump speaking was
delegated to Roosevelt, who traveled more than
21,000 miles, spoke in hundreds of towns and cities
throughout the country, and virtually mesmerized his
adoring audiences.

T.R.'s voice often cracked into a high falsetto,

and, near the end of the campaign, it was not much louder than a raspy whisper. But the beloved "Rough Rider" waved his arms vigorously and pounded his fists on podiums, impressing voters with his boundless energy, unbridled enthusiasm, and sincere devotion to the principles in which he believed. Never before in the nation's history had a vice presidential candidate so completely outshone the man at the head of the ticket.

The Republican candidates won a smashing victory over their Democratic opponents, and Roosevelt resigned himself to the boring role of vice president. He presided over Congress only a few months and then left for a vacation.

On September 6, 1901, the vice president learned that McKinley, while attending the Pan-American Exposition in Buffalo, New York, had been shot by an anarchist (a person opposed to all governments, rulers, and laws). Roosevelt rushed to the president's bedside but, told by the doctors that McKinley was recovering, T.R. left the president and traveled to the Adirondacks to do some hunting.

One week later, in the afternoon, Roosevelt was overtaken by a guide bringing the solemn news that the president was dying. T.R. took a 10-mile hike to the nearest road. Then followed, in the dead of night, a hazardous descent by horse and buggy down winding, pitch-black mountain roads that recently had been left muddy by heavy rains. Roosevelt reached the railroad station at five-thirty in the morning; there a special train was waiting to rush him to Buffalo. When he arrived in Buffalo, he was told that McKinley had died. Then he hastened to the nearby home of a friend, where on September 14, 1901, a judge administered the oath that made him the twenty-sixth president.

At the age of forty-two, Theodore Roosevelt was

the youngest man ever to become president. (John F. Kennedy was forty-three when he assumed office as the youngest *elected* president.)

Roosevelt assumed the presidency at a time of unprecedented economic and social ferment in the country, propelled by a growing progressive movement that called for the end of the abuses of industrial capitalism. In his first annual address to Congress in December 1901, the new president tried to strike a balance between free enterprise and the need to regulate, but not destroy, big business. He declared:

> *The captains of industry . . . have on the whole done great good to our people. Without them the material development of which we are so justly proud could never have taken place. . . . Yet it is also true that there are real and great evils. . . . There is a widespread conviction in the minds of the American people that the great corporations known as trusts are in certain of their features and tendencies hurtful to the general welfare. This . . . is based upon sincere conviction that combination and concentration should be, not prohibited, but supervised and within reasonable limits controlled; and in my judgment this conviction is right.*[8]

Six months after he moved into the White House, Roosevelt, through Attorney General Philander C. Knox, brought suit under the Sherman Antitrust Act of 1890 to dissolve the Northern Securities Company. This company had combined three railroads to monopolize transportation in the Northwest, which Roosevelt regarded as a conspiracy in restraint of trade. In 1904, by a five-to-four vote, the Supreme

Court agreed with the president and ordered the dissolution of the Northern Securities Company.

Later, the administration filed suits under the antitrust law against the United Steel Corporation, the Standard Oil Company, and other large combinations. In all, Roosevelt took legal action against forty-three companies, winning indictments in twenty-five cases, and earning him the title of "trust buster." The forceful president also enlisted the help of Congress in regulating big businesses. Congress passed the Elkins Act (1903), which made it illegal for railroads to give rebates (reduced shipping rates) to large customers. Congress also created a Department of Commerce and Labor (1903) to keep a watchful eye on businesses that might be engaged in practices harmful to the public.

In 1902 Roosevelt intervened dramatically in a major strike. Members of the United Mine Workers called a strike of 150,000 coal miners to obtain higher wages and better working conditions. The mine owners stubbornly refused to deal with the union. As winter approached and the possibility loomed that large numbers of Americans would be without the coal needed to heat their homes, the president threatened to call out troops to operate the mines in the interest of the public. The mine owners then agreed to arbitration, and Roosevelt appointed an impartial commission to investigate the dispute. It decided that the miners were entitled to a 10 percent wage increase and a shorter working day. The mine owners accepted these terms, and T.R. was widely applauded as a national leader who responded to the people's needs. Earlier presidents had sent troops to break up strikes, but none had used his office to help bring about a fair settlement of a labor dispute.

Roosevelt labeled his domestic reforms the "Square Deal." He said that his policies were intended to encourage fair play among all Americans, whether they were business owners or wage earners. All he wanted, he explained, was to see that every person had a square deal, no more and no less.

On the foreign front, Roosevelt said that his policy was to "speak softly but carry a big stick." But by "speaking softly" he did not mean that the United States should be only a timid spectator that did not become involved in affairs outside its borders. One area in which T.R. exhibited great interest was the Isthmus of Panama, where the United States wanted to build a canal linking the Atlantic to the Pacific. In 1903 Colombia, which then owned Panama, concluded a treaty with the United States leasing enough land on the Isthmus for the canal. But Colombia's legislature rejected the treaty, demanding more money for the land and claiming that the proposal to turn over some of its territory to another country was an insult to Colombia's sovereignty.

Roosevelt was infuriated by this turn of events, but his spirits brightened a short time later when a band of Panamanians rebelled against Colombian rule. The president wholeheartedly supported Panama's revolt, sending American naval vessels to the Isthmus to help prevent Colombian troops from suppressing the uprising. The Panamanian rebels proclaimed their independence, and three days later the United States recognized the infant republic. Within two weeks, the new Panamanian government agreed to a treaty whereby the United States leased a zone for the canal. Construction started on the huge ditch, and T.R. boasted about the aggressive role he played in laying the groundwork for an interocean canal. But not everyone applauded his rash action. His interference in Panama was an arrogant display of American power, and it left bitter feelings not only in Colombia but throughout most of Latin America.

Roosevelt wielded the "big stick" in other parts of Central and South America. In 1902 Germany and Great Britain blockaded ports in Venezuela in an effort to force payments of debts owed to them. When the debts still were not paid, the two European creditors threatened to seize Venezuelan customhouses and pay themselves out of the taxes as they collected them.

Feelings intensified when German naval vessels sank Venezuelan gunboats and bombarded Venezuelan ports. T.R. protested that such action was a violation of the Monroe Doctrine, and he warned the German ruler that any invasion of Venezuela would be met with force by the United States Navy. Roosevelt urged that the quarrel be settled peacefully, and finally, in 1903, this was done when the dispute was submitted to the International Court of Arbitration at the Hague, in the Netherlands.

In a somewhat similar situation in 1904, European nations sought to compel the Dominican Republic to pay its debts owed them. President Roosevelt agreed that the Dominicans must pay their debts, but he feared the intrusion of European power leveled at the island countries in the Caribbean Sea, which were near the United States. To deal with this threat, he proclaimed the Roosevelt Corollary to the Monroe Doctrine: it asserted that if force were needed to combat wrongdoing in the Western Hemisphere, it would be exerted by the United States acting in the role of an international police power. The president's critics charged that the Roosevelt Corollary ordered European countries to stay out of Latin America so that the United States could move in. But it achieved its immediate purpose: the Dominican government permitted the United States to collect its tariffs, paying 45 percent of the proceeds to the Dominicans and 55 percent to foreign creditors.

Roosevelt declared in 1904 that he would seek another term in the presidency. At the Republican convention he was nominated by acclamation on the first ballot. The Democrats, after failing to elect flamboyant William Jennings Bryan in either 1896 or 1900, chose as their 1904 presidential nominee a conservative, colorless judge, Alton B. Parker of the New York Court of Appeals. As expected, the enormously popular president won in a landslide, gaining a record-breaking margin of 2,543,695 votes. He carried every region of the country except the Democratic South.

All of the previous vice presidents who had ascended to the presidency in midterm—John Tyler, Millard Fillmore, Andrew Johnson, and Chester Alan Arthur—had been denied four more years in the White House. Theodore Roosevelt was the first of the accidental presidents to break this pattern and win a presidential election, which he did in a resounding fashion. The only thing that marred his victory was that on Election Night he made a statement that he later regretted: He said that after he had served the term to which he had just been elected, under no circumstances would he ever run again for president.

Whether he was in the White House or vacationing at Sagamore Hill, the family home on Oyster Bay in New York State, T.R. displayed the same vigor and enthusiasm in his private life that he demonstrated in his public career. He seldom slept more than five hours a night because there were so many things he was eager to do. He liked horseback riding, rowing, and swimming, and one of his favorite activities was what he called obstacle walks. He would gather friends and foreign diplomats for these walks through Rock Creek Park in Washington, D.C. First he would decide upon a final destination and then announce that every walker had to follow a straight path to that point, no matter what obstacles might be in the way. This sometimes required jumping over high bushes, scaling steep cliffs, and swimming in clothes across the creek, even when chunks of ice were floating in it.

The president was a tennis enthusiast, and he usually drew his opponents from a group of young government officials. The newspapers began referring to the group as the "tennis cabinet," and rumors circulated that any man who played tennis with Roosevelt had a bright political future ahead. T.R. played an unorthodox brand of tennis: he gripped the racket halfway up the handle and, because of his poor eyesight, instead of throwing the ball into the air when he served, he held it in his left hand and hit it between his fingers. Although his hand usually was sore after a match, Roosevelt played the game so hard that he often was victorious.

Long after his college days, T.R. continued boxing. As governor of New York he had sparred twice a week with Mike Donovan, a former middleweight boxing champion. On the evening before his inauguration for a four-year term as president, Roosevelt and Donovan had a bruising ten-round match. When he climbed onto the mat, T.R. told the ex-champion, "Now, Mike, we must have a good bout this evening. It will brighten me for tomorrow, which will be a trying day."[9]

The president boxed frequently in the White House with young prizefighters from the Army. Then one day an Army captain landed a stinging blow that caused Roosevelt to suffer a detached retina and lose the sight in his left eye. He kept this injury a secret and had to give up boxing. Instead, the robust president turned first to wrestling and then to jujitsu.

One of the many hats that Roosevelt enjoyed

wearing was that of a conciliator. In 1905 college football was on the verge of extinction because the game had become so rough that it caused many serious injuries and even deaths. Roosevelt called to the White House the athletic officials of many colleges and warned them that football had to be made safer. The next year new rules were drawn up that outlawed the most brutal aspects of the game.

In the same year, at Portsmouth, New Hampshire, the president brought together diplomats from Japan and Russia, which had been warring over control of Manchuria and Korea. A peace treaty was signed, and for his service in helping to end the Russo-Japanese War, Roosevelt was awarded the 1906 Nobel Peace Prize. He was the first president to be honored with this award.

One of President Roosevelt's chief concerns was the conservation and wise use of land and natural resources. The Reclamation Act of 1902 authorized the spending of money from the sale of land in sixteen semiarid western states for irrigation purposes. Under this law, huge dams were constructed and the task of reclaiming unproductive dry areas in the West was begun.

In an era when the public showed little interest in protecting the environment for future generations, Roosevelt took several other bold steps. He withdrew 125 million acres of timberland from sale, setting aside much of this land as national forests. He doubled the number of national parks, established fifty game preserves, and founded sixteen national monuments.

In 1908 the first White House conference on the conservation of natural resources was held. Governors, university presidents, scientists, and businessmen met together to consider policies to preserve the nation's resources. Following the conference, a National Conservation Commission was established, and forty-one states soon started their own conservation agencies.

Roosevelt's second term saw the continuation of his reform policies. The Hepburn Act of 1906 strengthened the Interstate Commerce Commission in several ways. It gave the commission the power to fix railroad rates and widened its jurisdiction to include express cars, sleeping-car companies, pipelines, terminals, and ferries. It prevented railroads from operating other businesses, such as coal mining, and it abolished free passes on railroads to anyone except employees.

In 1906 the president signed two laws that protected consumers. One was the Pure Food and Drug Act, prohibiting the manufacture, sale, or interstate transportation of adulterated (impure) foods, drugs, medicines, or liquor, and requiring honest labeling of ingredients. The other act provided for regular inspection of animals at stockyards and meat at packing houses.

T.R. was determined that other countries must recognize the United States as a first-rate world power, and to this end he pushed through Congress appropriation bills to strengthen the army and navy. Roosevelt also decided to send a battle fleet on a cruise around the world to demonstrate his belief that peace was best served through a show of strength. At that time, relations with Japan were strained, and there was fear that a Japanese military buildup was aimed at the United States. Some hesitant congressmen insisted that the fleet could not sail because they had not voted the money needed for the voyage. The president replied sharply that he had enough money to get the ships to the Pacific, and Congress would have to pay for their return.

Sixteen battleships and 12,000 men set out on

this mission in late 1907. The first foreign ports where the fleet would stop were in Japan, and there was concern that the Japanese might resent the fleet's visit and regard it as a belligerent act. But the Japanese people greeted the American sailors warmly. A short time later, the fleet continued its cruise, finally returning home in February 1909. The president was proud of this accomplishment, calling it an important contribution to world peace.

When Roosevelt's tenure in the White House ended, he picked as his successor William Howard Taft, the secretary of war and a close personal friend. The Republican convention confirmed this selection, and in the 1908 election Taft easily defeated William Jennings Bryan, the Democrats' only three-time loser in the presidential sweepstakes.

Only fifty years old when he stepped down from the presidency, Roosevelt still was energetic and ambitious. He sensed that he had reached the pinnacle of his political career too soon; nothing else could be as exciting or rewarding as serving his country on the rung of the political ladder that provided the most power and generated the most publicity.

The former president tried to turn his back on politics by embarking on a strenuous hunting trip to Africa. He had been on many hunting expeditions before. In the West he had sought buffalo, caribou, moose, cougars, and wolves. In a trip to the South for bear, he told a reporter that he had spotted a cub which was too young to shoot. When the newspapers publicized this incident, the term "teddy bear" was born.

Roosevelt's African expedition, which was sponsored by the Smithsonian Institution, lasted a year and included taxidermists and naturalists. Roosevelt bagged more than 500 animals and birds; some of the species were so rare that they had never before been represented in the Smithsonian collection. When the former president emerged from Africa, he toured Europe and was entertained by the royalty of many countries.

On his return to Sagamore Hill, Roosevelt wrote another book, *African Game Trails,* and magazine articles. But inevitably his attention was drawn back to the political arena, and he began expressing strong criticism of President Taft, who he felt was not continuing his progressive policies. As the 1912 presidential election drew near, many of Roosevelt's friends urged him to run again, and the restless ex-president responded to their advice by triumphantly declaring, "My hat is in the ring."

There was no question that Roosevelt was more popular with voters than Taft was. He defeated Taft in nine of the ten Republican primaries in which they were the principal candidates. But the Taft forces controlled the party machinery at the Republican convention, and they dictated the nomination of the president for a second term. Roosevelt, however, was not content to give up the battle and dutifully support the G.O.P. (Republican) candidate. Instead, two months after the Republicans had rejected his bid, he was nominated for the presidency by the Progressive party at a convention charged with intense emotion and pulsating excitement. T.R. was so exultant that he spread his lips in his famous toothy grin and exclaimed to reporters, "I'm feeling like a Bull Moose!"[10] From that time on, the bull moose was the Progressive party's symbol.

On October 14, 1912, during the campaign, Roosevelt was getting into a car to go to an auditorium in Milwaukee where he was scheduled to speak, when a fanatic shot him in the chest. Aides wanted to rush the former president to a hospital immediately, but he brushed them aside with the command

112

that he would go ahead and deliver his address. With blood gushing from his wound, T.R. spoke to a stunned audience for over an hour. Then he went to a hospital, where he recuperated for about two weeks. The bullet that had struck the ex-president was never removed because it had not entered a vital organ. Fortunately, it had been slowed by the doubled-over pages of his prepared speech and a metal glasses case in his breast pocket, so it came to rest a short distance from his right lung.

In the election, Roosevelt outpolled Taft in both the electoral vote and the popular vote, but the Republican forces were split so badly that Democrat Woodrow Wilson emerged the victor. Because of Roosevelt's strong showing, however, this was the only time since the formation of the Republican party that its presidential candidate did not finish in either first or second place.

In 1913 Roosevelt embarked on a seven-month, 1,500-mile expedition into the Amazon Basin of Brazil. He explored a tributary of the Amazon River, which was called the River of Doubt because its treacherous rapids and whirlpools had defied previous explorers attempting to chart its course. T.R.'s expedition provided so much new information about this river that it was renamed Rio Roosevelt. But his experience in the hot, humid Amazon rain forest nearly cost Roosevelt his life. He contracted malaria and became delirious with a fever that ran as high as 105 degrees. He also cut his leg on a jagged rock in the river, and a serious infection developed. After several days when his life hung in the balance, T.R. regained enough strength to travel home, but he never fully recovered from the illnesses that struck him on this trip.

Nevertheless, the ailing former president still was driven to lead a strenuous life. He vigorously sought the Republican nomination for the presidency in 1916, but his defection from the party in 1912 had offended many G O P leaders, who regarded him as an outcast and refused to run him for president again. When World War I started in Europe, T.R. repeatedly spoke out for American preparedness, and he savagely attacked President Wilson's neutrality policy as a weak, timid response to German aggression.

As soon as the United States entered the war in April 1917, Roosevelt hurried to Washington to offer his services. He urged President Wilson to let him enlist a volunteer regiment, as he had done in the Spanish-American War. But Wilson turned down his offer, and T.R. had to follow the course of the war from the sidelines. His four sons, however, were all in active service. Quentin, his youngest son, was a pilot and lost his life when his plane was shot down by the Germans. This deeply saddened the former president, whose spirits never completely revived after this tragedy.

Besides recurrences of the malaria and leg infection that he had contracted in Brazil, in his last years Roosevelt was plagued by painful inflammatory rheumatism and deafness in one ear. On January 6, 1919, he suffered a heart attack and died in his sleep. He was buried at a cemetery near his beloved Sagamore Hill home.

Theodore Roosevelt at times appeared rash and arrogant, and there is no doubt that he adored being cast as the star performer on center stage. Modesty and a willingness to share the limelight with others were qualities that he usually brushed aside. As one observer pointed out, T.R. insisted on being "the bride at every wedding, the corpse at every funeral."[11]

In an age not yet introduced to the horror of atomic weapons, he reveled in the supposed glory of warfare and pursued foreign policies that often were openly aggressive and belligerent. He treated smaller countries, like Colombia and the Dominican Republic, as inferior neighbors. And he was not afraid to threaten large nations, as exemplified by his condemnation of Germany in the Venezuelan debt controversy and, after World War I started in Europe, by his warlike attitude toward Germany while the United States was still at peace with that country.

Still, it must be remembered that Roosevelt's rise to the presidency occurred at the same time in history that the United States was emerging as one of the most powerful and wealthiest nations in the world. If T.R. was brashly asserting America's newfound strength at the turn of this century, he was merely the spokesman of a heady, optimistic people who rejoiced that they no longer had to play second fiddle to anyone. Perhaps the British writer John Morley put it most succinctly when, after a visit to the White House in 1903, he declared, "Roosevelt is not an American, you know. He is America."[12]

In the field of domestic reform, Roosevelt achieved an enviable record. He was the first president to fight the trusts and monopolies that were strangling competition in many businesses. His administration attacked railroad abuses and defended consumer causes, such as the need for coal to heat homes and the safety of food and drugs. And T.R. took unprecedented steps in implementing the conservation of natural resources and the preservation of national forests and parks for later generations to enjoy.

From the time he was an infant who struggled against bouts of asthma until he passed away at age sixty, T.R. was always a battler. "Death had to take him sleeping," observed Vice President Thomas R. Marshall, "for if Roosevelt had been awake, there would have been a fight."[13]

Chapter 7
Calvin Coolidge:
The Silent President

In the tiny hamlet of Plymouth Notch, Vermont, Calvin Coolidge was born on the Fourth of July in 1872. Plymouth Notch consisted of a general store owned by Calvin's father, John, a school, a church, and seven farmhouses. It was a short distance east of the town of Plymouth, which had a population of about 1,300. Calvin and his sister, Abigail, were born in a house that adjoined their father's store.

John Coolidge earned some of his living from the store and some from farming. In addition to holding these two jobs, he found time for public service. He was elected to the board that governed Plymouth, and he became a justice of the peace and notary public. John Coolidge served six years in the Vermont House of Representatives and one term in the Vermont Senate. At the age of three Calvin was taken to the state capital at Montpelier to watch his father take part in the legislature.

Like most other Vermont farm boys in the 1800s, young Coolidge had little time for carefree play and idleness. He was awake before dawn, dressed in a cold room, and then went to the kitchen to wash in cold water. There were chores to do before school, after school, on weekends, and during vacations. Firewood had to be split and stacked in boxes, fields had to be plowed and planted in corn, fruit had to be picked, and maple trees had to be tapped for their syrup. His father used to tell friends that Calvin could get more sap out of a maple tree than any other boy his size.

Coaxing a living out of New England's stony soil was hard, monotonous, lonely work. But it taught Calvin to be self-reliant, thrifty, and solemn—qualities that became integral parts of his personality for the rest of his life. Seldom did he call on anyone for a favor or to help with a task for which he was responsible. He was so frugal with money that acquaintances often regarded him as a stingy penny-pincher, and so thrifty with words that he earned the nickname "Silent Cal." Usually his manner was sober, sometimes even gruff, yet he had a dry wit that evoked chuckles and laughter from those who were treated to his humorous remarks.

Calvin, a freckled redhead with blue eyes and a long, thin nose, went to the local, two-room school until the age of thirteen. Then he studied at Black River Academy, a private school in Ludlow, 12 miles from home. In 1891 he entered Amherst College in Massachusetts. His grades during his first two years of college were average, but in his junior and senior years his work improved, and he graduated with honors. At college Calvin took no part in sports; he did not particularly enjoy athletics, and also he had a slight build and suffered from frequent attacks of asthma.

Even though his classmates considered him a campus wit, Calvin had few college friends because he didn't talk much and was painfully shy. This tendency to be a loner continued into his mature years, which was very unusual for a man who spent most of his adult life in the backslapping, wheeler-dealer arena of politics. Coolidge was keenly aware of his reserved, standoffish nature and once explained:

> *When I was a little fellow, as long ago as I*
> *can remember, I would go into a panic if I*
> *heard strange voices in the kitchen. I felt I*
> *just couldn't meet the people and shake hands*
> *with them. . . . The hardest thing in the*
> *world was to have to go through the kitchen door*
> *and give them a greeting. I was almost ten before*
> *I realized I couldn't go on that way. And by*
> *fighting hard I used to manage to get through that*
> *door. I'm all right with old friends, but every*
> *time I meet a stranger, I've got to go through the*
> *old kitchen door, back home, and it's not easy.*[1]

After graduating from college, Coolidge moved to Northampton, Massachusetts, where he studied law in the office of a legal firm. He was admitted to the bar in 1897 and began practicing law in Northampton, which he called his home for the remainder of his life. In 1898 he launched his political career by running successfully for a seat on the Northampton City Council. In 1901 he became city solicitor (chief law officer) of Northampton, and in 1903 he was named clerk of the courts for Hampshire County.

Northampton was the site of the Clarke Institute for the Deaf. One morning Grace Ann Goodhue, a teacher at the institute, was sprinkling the flowers in front of the school. When she happened to look up at an open window in the boardinghouse next door, she saw a strange sight. There stood a young man in long underwear shaving—and wearing a hat! Grace laughed spontaneously and then quickly turned away to continue watering the plants. Coolidge heard her laughter and asked to be introduced to Grace. At their first meeting the embarrassed young man explained that he had a troublesome cowlick that would lie flat on his head only if he pressed it into place with a hat each morning.

Calvin and Grace began seeing each other often, and they were married the following year. The Coolidges had two sons, John and Calvin, Jr.

Grace Coolidge's personality was as different from Calvin's as day is from night. She was an extrovert—a friendly, outgoing person who enjoyed meeting people and made them feel comfortable. She was undoubtedly a strong asset to the political career of her introverted husband.

Republican Coolidge was elected in 1906 and reelected the next year to the lower house of the Massachusetts legislature. After serving two terms there he decided to run for mayor of Northampton. The race against the Democratic nominee was close, but Coolidge squeaked through by the slight margin of 187 votes. In his two terms as mayor, 1909–1912, he expanded the fire and police departments, secured an increase in teachers' pay, and improved streets and sidewalks. But in spite of these expenditures, by shrewd, efficient management of funds he was able to lower the tax rate and even reduce the city's debt almost by half.

In 1912 Coolidge was elected to the first of four terms in the state Senate. Although he belonged to the conservative wing of the Republican party, Senator Coolidge supported much progressive legislation. He championed several measures to help women, including women's suffrage (the right to vote), aid to needy mothers, pensions for women, and a minimum wage for women workers. He also voted for a

119

state income tax, legalization of picketing, the direct election of United States senators, and workmen's injury compensation. Yet Coolidge declared very emphatically that his political creed was based on economy and efficiency in government. He favored some political and social reforms, but primarily those that would not cost the taxpayers much money.[2]

Coolidge served as lieutenant governor of Massachusetts from 1916 through 1918, and then in 1919 he was elected governor. The quiet, antisocial politician from Plymouth Notch felt that the office of governor was the highest political position he would ever hold, and he worked to compile a good record for his administration. Coolidge encouraged the enactment of laws limiting the work week of women and children to forty-eight hours, prohibiting unfair practices by landlords, raising workmen's compensation allowances, and regulating outdoor advertising. And he urged increases in pay for teachers, factory workers, and the Boston police force.

If Coolidge had been successful in satisfying the needs of the Boston police, he probably never would have become president. Unable to obtain higher wages and better working conditions through regular channels, the police force decided to press its demands by forming a union and joining the American Federation of Labor (AFL). This infuriated the police commissioner, who proclaimed that police officers cannot belong to a union and still perform their peacekeeping duties. Quickly he suspended nineteen members of the police officers' union. This rash action was applauded by many Bostonians who were suspicious of union motives. At that time the country was in the midst of a frightening "Red Scare," and large numbers of Americans feared that the epidemic of strikes breaking out in various industries was masterminded by Communists.

120

The next day, September 9, 1919, most of the Boston police walked off the job. That night there was looting and rioting in the city. Terrified citizens stayed in their homes, latching the doors and drawing curtains across the windows. The mayor of Boston got in touch with Coolidge and asked him to call out the state guard to restore law and order. But the governor hesitated to step in; he preferred letting the local authorities settle the issue.

The city officials desperately tried to recruit an amateur police force made up of volunteer state guardsmen, ex-servicemen from World War I, and Harvard students. But a second night of violence occurred. Finally, Coolidge summoned the state guard and ordered it to patrol the streets of Boston. Samuel Gompers, president of the AFL, then sent a telegram to the Massachusetts governor, imploring him to overrule the police commissioner, reinstate the suspended police officers, and let them keep their union.

Coolidge wired back: "There is no right to strike against the public safety by anybody, anywhere, anytime."[3] The news services picked up this blunt statement, and it was printed on the front pages of papers across the land. President Woodrow Wilson and 70,000 others flooded the State House in Boston with messages praising Coolidge's bold stand. Overnight, the drab Massachusetts governor had attained national fame and become a hero in many households.

When the Republican national convention assembled in June 1920, Coolidge's name was placed in nomination as a favorite-son candidate for the presidency. He received thirty-four votes on the first ballot, even though he had done nothing to promote his candidacy. Several other Republicans, however, had waged active campaigns for the nomination and extensively courted the delegates. A deadlock developed in which none of the front-running candidates could win a majority of delegate votes. So, on the tenth ballot, the Republicans finally gave the nomination to a compromise, dark-horse contender, Senator Warren G. Harding of Ohio.

Harding was an amiable, likable, handsome politician, but his record in the Senate was at best mediocre. Even his strongest supporters conceded that Harding was not likely to become a great president, but as one of them put it: "There ain't any first-raters this year . . . . We got a lot of second-raters and Warren Harding is the best of the second-raters."[4]

A small group of powerful senators, led by convention chairman Senator Henry Cabot Lodge of Massachusetts, had played a large role in determining that Harding would be the party's standard-bearer. This same Senate clique decided that another senator, Irvine Lenroot of Wisconsin, would be Harding's running mate. Lenroot's name was routinely placed before the convention, and many delegates, regarding his nomination as a certainty, began heading for the exits. The convention had dragged on for four days in sweltering Chicago, and the weary, perspiring Republicans were eager to start home.

Suddenly a man in the Oregon delegation, standing on a chair, shouted frantically for recognition. When the convention chairman decided to let him have his say, Wallace McCamant, an Oregon judge, delivered a brief nominating speech for Coolidge. A large number of delegates, eager for an opportunity to revolt against the bosses who had dictated Harding's nomination for the presidency, spontaneously burst into applause and called out the name of the popular "law-and-order" governor. On the first roll call they selected Coolidge to be Harding's running mate.

Calvin and Grace Coolidge were preparing to go to dinner in Boston when the telephone rang. The governor picked up the receiver and learned, much to his surprise, that he was the Republicans' choice for vice president. When he conveyed this unexpected development to his wife, she said, "You aren't going to take it, are you?" Coolidge looked at his wife and stoically replied, "I suppose I'll have to."[5]

The Republican party platform called for the reduction of spending by the federal government and continued support for a protective tariff. But it straddled the most important issue of the day—whether the United States should join the new League of Nations. The Republican-controlled Senate had refused to ratify the Treaty of Versailles, which included membership in the League, partly because the treaty was inspired chiefly by Democratic President Woodrow Wilson and partly because of a fear that the League would limit American sovereignty. Some prominent Republicans, like former President William Howard Taft and former Supreme Court Justice Charles Evans Hughes, supported United States participation in the League, but many others did not. So the party platform sidestepped this controversial question, stating vaguely that "the Republican party stands for agreement among the nations to preserve the peace of the world."[6]

Meanwhile, the Democrats nominated for president Governor James M. Cox of Ohio and for vice president Franklin D. Roosevelt, the thirty-eight-year-old assistant secretary of the navy. Shortly after the convention, Cox and Roosevelt called on President Wilson, who was partially paralyzed from a stroke, and assured him they would carry his crusade for the League of Nations from one end of the country to the other. The Democratic candidates kept this promise. Cox traveled 22,000 miles and spoke to two million people; Roosevelt covered almost as much ground and delivered an average of ten speeches a day.

Harding and Coolidge, on the other hand, were less energetic candidates. For much of the campaign, Harding stayed at home in Marion, Ohio, greeting visitors from his front porch and expounding on his theme, "Return to Normalcy," in a few well-rehearsed remarks. He promised to lead the nation back to the "good old times" of the late nineteenth century when there were no worries about world wars and international organizations, personal sacrifices and wartime shortages, high taxes and inflation, Communists and "Red Scares," and gangsterism and loose morals.

Coolidge, seldom an effective speaker because of his harsh nasal twang and monotonous delivery, echoed Harding's message. The Massachusetts governor's campaign was mainly limited to his native New England and a short trip into the Solid South, which was almost certain to vote Democratic because it had supported Democratic candidates since the end of Reconstruction.

On Election Day, the ticket of Harding and Coolidge won a landslide victory, with a record-shattering 60.2 percent of the popular vote and a plurality of nearly 7 million votes. Carrying the entire North and West, as well as some of the border states of the South, the Republican candidates won 404 electoral votes to 127 for their Democratic opponents. (Coolidge's victory over Roosevelt for the vice presidency marked the only time in FDR's political career that he lost an election.)

When the presidential election was over, Harding set a precedent by asking the vice president to sit as an official member of the cabinet. Coolidge accepted the invitation, but he made few contributions

124

to cabinet meetings. The vice president presided routinely over the Senate, seldom expressing any opinions from the chair. Once, when asked to use his power of recognition to permit a certain senator to speak on the floor, he knew that this would displease another senator, so he simply avoided making a decision. At the critical moment, he handed the gavel to one of the senators, left the chamber, and did not return until the question was resolved.

Harding's administration was plagued by scandal and corruption. The most damaging misdeeds were the Teapot Dome and Elk Hills scandals, involving the secretary of the interior, who had leased government-owned oil lands to private parties in return for huge bribes. The head of the Veterans Bureau also had been dishonest; he had arranged fraudulent contracts that cost the taxpayers an estimated $200 million. The alien property custodian was another Harding appointee who had accepted bribes, and Attorney General Harry Daugherty, Harding's closest adviser and confidante, was accused of dishonest dealings.

Evidence of some of these criminal acts came to Harding's attention; the president was both angry and despondent when he discovered that he had been betrayed by close friends he had put in high offices. Hoping that a change of scenery would improve his spirits and perhaps lower his high blood pressure, the troubled president embarked on a railroad trip to Alaska. His train made frequent stops, and Harding used these occasions to talk about his policies to the crowds that gathered, eager to catch a glimpse of the well-liked president. (The public was as yet unaware of the corruption in Harding's administration, but his reputation soon would be badly tarnished when news reporters got hold of the shameful stories involving his associates.)

On his return trip south, Harding was scheduled to spend a short time in San Francisco. Tired and feeling ill, he checked into the Palace Hotel. After a couple of days of rest, he felt better and planned to resume his trip the following day. But while he was lying on his bed and his wife was reading a magazine article to him, the president suddenly suffered a massive stroke and died that night, August 2, 1923.

Vice President Coolidge was spending his summer vacation at his father's home in Plymouth Notch, Vermont. On the night of Harding's death, Coolidge went to bed at his customary hour of nine o'clock. Getting word to the vice president was no easy matter, as the Coolidge home had no telephone. The nearest telephone linking the rustic area to the modern world was at Bridgewater, 12 miles away. Shortly after one o'clock a courier from Bridgewater drove quickly over the bumpy country roads and woke the elder Coolidge to inform him that his son, Calvin, was about to become president of the United States.

The old storekeeper-farmer climbed upstairs, calling in a trembling voice, "Calvin! Calvin!" While Calvin and Grace Coolidge dressed hurriedly, the former farm boy who was soon to become chief executive turned to his wife and said confidently, "I believe I can swing it."[7]

After his father lit the kerosene lamps in the parlor, Calvin studied a copy of the Constitution to determine what qualifications were needed to receive the presidential oath. He decided that this oath was the same as the one he had taken as vice president. Since his father was a notary public and justice of the peace, he was empowered to administer the oath. Placing his hand on the family Bible, Calvin Coolidge became the first and only president to be sworn into office by his father.

Shortly after Coolidge moved into the White

House, a Senate subcommittee investigation began bringing to public attention the sordid details of the Teapot Dome and Elk Hills scandals. Newspapers also started revealing the fraudulent acts committed by other members of Harding's inner circle in the executive department. None of this corruption was ever directly linked to Harding or to his vice president, who had a reputation for unimpeachable honesty. When Coolidge became president, he replaced the tainted officials in the administration with men of unquestioned integrity.

On December 6, 1923, Coolidge delivered his first message to Congress. (This was the first official presidential speech to be broadcast on radio.) He called for support of the World Court but for continued aloofness from the League of Nations. Coolidge also restated his well-known convictions that taxes should be reduced and economy practiced by the federal government.

Congress clashed with Coolidge over the Soldiers' Bonus Bill in May 1924. The bill awarded World War I veterans bonuses for their wartime service, to be paid twenty years later at an approximate cost of $2 billion. President Coolidge believed this measure called for too large a federal expenditure, so he vetoed it. But Congress passed the bill again, by more than a two-thirds margin in each house, thus overriding the president's veto.

In the same month, Congress passed a sweeping immigration bill designed to control entrance into the United States. Between 1890 and 1910 large numbers of immigrants had poured into the country from lands in southern and eastern Europe. Some prejudiced Americans objected to these newcomers because they often were Catholics or Jews, many having come from poor, illiterate peasant families. So the Immigration Bill of 1924 rolled back the quotas of new immigrants to only 2 percent of the number of each nationality that was in the United States in 1890, thereby sharply reducing the flow of aliens from southern and eastern Europe. It excluded Japanese immigrants entirely. President Coolidge signed this bill into law.

"Silent Cal" had been chief executive less than a year when the Republican convention assembled to name its ticket for the 1924 presidential and vice presidential races. Coolidge was easily nominated on the first ballot, garnering 1,065 of the 1,109 delegate votes. Former Budget Director Charles G. Dawes of Illinois was chosen as the vice presidential nominee.

The recent revelations of corruption in high Republican circles should have boosted the Democrats' chances in the 1924 election (just as the Watergate affair did a half century later). But the Democrats muffed this golden opportunity at their convention, mainly because they spent most of their time fighting among themselves instead of uniting on a single candidate and a party platform. Divisive conflicts emerged between delegates from the urban East and those from the rural South and West, and seventeen names were placed in nomination for the presidency. Nine days of heated debates were consumed before a compromise candidate finally was chosen on a record-breaking 103rd ballot. He was John W. Davis of West Virginia, a little-known conservative Wall Street lawyer.

Since both the Republicans and Democrats had selected conservative candidates, dissatisfied liberals and progressives felt they could not vote for either nominee. Seeing an opportunity to develop a farmer-labor movement, they held their own convention and nominated Senator Robert M. LaFollette of Wisconsin as the standard-bearer of the Progressive party. Their party platform favored using the power of the federal government to crush private monopoly. It also endorsed public ownership of the nation's water supply, major natural resources, and railroads. It supported an increase in the inheritance tax, the abolition of court injunctions to prevent strikes, and a federal law to protect children in industry.

When Coolidge's opponents took to the stump, they criticized his administration for neglecting important economic and social problems. But their verbal attacks failed to evoke strong responses from "Silent Cal" or change his fundamental belief that the American people needed less government rather than more. The president refused to take an active role in his own campaign. He let other Republicans do most of the speaking for him until the last week of the contest, when he emerged from virtual isolation to deliver a pro-business speech to an appreciative audience at the U.S. Chamber of Commerce.

Nor did Coolidge respond often to the questions of reporters covering the campaign. One newsman described his futile attempt to pin down the president on current issues. "Will you say something about unemployment?" the reporter asked. "No," replied Coolidge. "Will you tell us your views about the world situation?" persisted the reporter. "No." "About your message to Congress?" "No." The disappointed reporter started to leave, but as he reached the door, Coolidge said, "Wait." The newsman hoped that the president finally was about to make some important comment, but instead Coolidge cautioned him: "Now remember—don't quote me."[8]

The quiet president became even more withdrawn and less talkative after a tragic family accident occurred during the election campaign. Coolidge's youngest son, Calvin, Jr., blistered a toe while playing tennis in sneakers without socks. An infection developed, and the boy died at the age of sixteen.

(Antibiotics had not yet been developed.) Years later Coolidge wrote in his autobiography that after young Calvin's death the power and glory of the presidency no longer were meaningful to him.

As Election Day approached, prosperity appeared to be reigning, the country was at peace, and many people felt secure under the leadership of the frugal, tight-lipped, no-nonsense president. The popular slogan "Keep Cool with Coolidge" reflected the sentiments of a majority of voters. Coolidge was elected by a substantial margin, gaining 15,717,553 popular votes (54 percent) compared to 8,386,169 votes (28.8 percent) for Davis and 4,814,050 votes (16.56 percent) for LaFollette. The president carried thirty-five states with 382 electoral votes, Davis won twelve states with 136 electoral votes, LaFollette took only his home state of Wisconsin with 13 electoral votes. (Following in the footsteps of Theodore Roosevelt, Coolidge became the second accidental president elected to a full four-year term.)

Coolidge maintained a relaxed, leisurely attitude toward his job in the White House. He usually slept eight to nine hours each night and often took a two-hour nap after lunch. Most of the ordinary problems of administration he delegated to his staff and department heads, and the president often avoided or delayed taking action on important matters. "If you see ten troubles coming down the road," he explained, "you can be sure that nine will run into the ditch before they reach you and you have to battle with only one of them."[9]

Social engagements were of little interest to the introverted president, but protocol required him to attend a number of official functions and some parties. A favorite story tells about the time he was seated next to a hostess who had bet a friend that she could coax him to say at least three words. All during dinner she tried various ways to draw the president into a conversation, but all her efforts failed. Finally, in desperation, she told him, "I made a bet today that I could get more than two words out of you." Coolidge looked at her glumly and retorted, "You lose."[10]

Grace Coolidge's sparkling personality kept life at the White House from becoming utterly bleak and grim. Her warmth and graciousness made her a popular First Lady with both the press and the public. Among her many interests during her years in the nation's capital, she became an avid fan of the Washington Senators baseball team. She went to games as often as possible and listened to others on the radio.

Her husband did not like baseball, but Grace prevailed upon him to take her to the opening game of the 1924 World Series between the Senators and the New York Giants. When the score was tied at the end of the ninth inning, the president rose to leave, but Mrs. Coolidge clutched at Calvin's coattails and begged him to sit back down. He solemnly agreed and watched the rest of the game with bored indifference, while his wife helped cheer the Washington team to an exciting victory.

Business rather than politics made the big news of the Coolidge era. Industry was flourishing, and corporations became larger through both growth and consolidation. Thousands of companies merged, and advertising reached a new peak, helping to sell the huge quantities of merchandise produced by the factories. Many cities and towns enjoyed real estate booms, and the stock market kept spiraling upward.

President Coolidge put his faith in the development of business as the most likely means of leading Americans to permanent prosperity, individual development, self-reliance, and social progress. This point of view was clearly expressed in his famous statement that "the chief business of America is business." To promote business interests, the Coolidge administration enlisted the support of Congress, which passed bills sharply reducing income and inheritance taxes. Congress also eliminated federal gift taxes and most of the excise taxes (a type of sales tax) imposed during World War I. High tariffs were continued to protect American industry, while regulation of businesses was relaxed. Furthermore, Coolidge fought against most federal projects that would have drained money from the treasury, and his economy measures reduced the national debt about a billion dollars a year.

Unfortunately, "Coolidge Prosperity" stood on unsteady legs. The wealth of the nation was distributed very unevenly. By the end of the Coolidge administration, 5 percent of the population received nearly one-third of all personal income. While industrial workers' wages increased, the prices they paid for goods increased even faster. Farmers faced an even worse plight. The high tariff wall that the United States had erected prevented other countries from selling their goods to Americans. In turn, those countries did not have the money with which to buy food from American farmers. So our farmers were saddled with a huge surplus of food products that could not be sold at a fair price, and thousands of farms were lost because the families that owned them could not pay their debts.

President Coolidge, however, took no effective steps that might have lessened the problems of city workers or farmers. Congress proposed the McNary-Haugen Bill to help farmers. It would have raised farm prices by setting up a government corporation to buy surplus crops for resale abroad and then either store them until prices rose on the world market or sell them at a loss. Twice the bill passed, and twice the president vetoed it. Farmers, he insisted, should work out their own problems.

The endless skyrocketing of the stock market during the Coolidge administration worried the financial community. Much of the wild speculation was based on brokers' loans to investors. When these loans climbed to the astronomical height of $4 billion in 1928, economists warned the president that unless there was some regulation of the stock market, it could be heading toward a disastrous fall that might accelerate a severe depression. Coolidge responded confidently that the brokers' loans were not too large; he pointed out that bank deposits and the number of stocks offered for sale were on the rise too. Furthermore, the president declared that regulation of the New York Stock Exchange was the responsibility of New York State, not of the federal government.

Little was accomplished in international developments during the Coolidge presidency. The Senate voted in 1926 for the United States to join the World Court, but this did not occur because the Senate coupled our admission to the Court with reservations (amendments) that were not accepted by other nations. Like Harding, Coolidge opposed United States participation in the League of Nations. And he insisted that our Allies in World War I pay back all the money they borrowed from us to fight the war, even though their economies were suffering severe hardships.

In 1928, with Coolidge's approval, a treaty to outlaw war was drawn up by Secretary of State Frank B. Kellogg and French Foreign Minister Aristide Briand. Eventually sixty-two nations signed the treaty, agreeing to renounce war as a means of settling international disputes. But the Kellogg-Briand Pact included no provisions for enforcement, so it failed to prevent wars from breaking out.

Some political observers believed that Coolidge would seek another four-year term in the presidency, but in the summer of 1927 he handed reporters a brief statement saying that he did not choose to run for president in 1928. After leaving the White House, he retired to Northampton, Massachusetts, where he wrote his autobiography, magazine articles, and a daily newspaper column. On January 5, 1933, he suffered a heart attack and died.

There were serious errors and significant weaknesses in the Coolidge administration. The president turned a deaf ear to the pressing needs of farmers, industrial workers, and World War I veterans. He supported an immigration act that discriminated sharply against aliens from some parts of Europe and Japan. And he failed to heed the warnings of economists that bold action was needed to curb the stock market speculation. Less than eight months after Coolidge left the presidency, the market crashed, setting off a wave of interrelated economic hardships, such as unemployment and overproduction, that soon led to the Great Depression.

Criticism can also be leveled at Coolidge for his isolationist approach to foreign affairs. By insisting that the United States—the world's most powerful and wealthiest country—should not belong to the League of Nations, Coolidge was badly crippling that organization's capacity to accomplish its goal of maintaining peace. By endorsing high tariffs and the forced payment of war debts from our former Allies, Coolidge was contributing to the disruption of foreign trade and the economic distress of other countries.

Nevertheless, there were some positive aspects of the Coolidge administration. He restored the integrity and honesty of the executive branch of the government after the sordid Harding scandals. Also, he presided over a period of enormous business expansion, due in part to his urging Congress to lower taxes, eliminate regulations, and reduce the national budget.

Coolidge's business-oriented accomplishments greatly impressed another conservative president, who served more than a half century later in the White House. One of Ronald Reagan's first symbolic acts after he assumed the presidency in 1981 was to hang a portrait of Coolidge in the White House Cabinet Room.

"Look at his record," Reagan said of Coolidge. "He cut the taxes four times. We had probably the greatest growth and prosperity that we've ever known. I have taken heed of that because if he did that by doing nothing, maybe that's the answer."[11]

Chapter 8
Harry S Truman:
Man from Missouri

When their first child was born on May 8, 1884, in
Lamar, Missouri, Martha and John Truman named
him Harry after a maternal uncle, Harrison Young.
But they were undecided whether to give him the
middle name Shippe, after his paternal grandfather,
Anderson Shippe Truman, or Solomon, after his
maternal grandfather, Solomon Young. So they
compromised and honored both grandparents by
giving Harry the letter S as his full middle name.

John Truman was a farmer and livestock trader.
During Harry's first few years the family moved frequently from one farming area to another. They finally settled on a farm on the outskirts of Independence, Missouri, not far from Kansas City. There
Harry attended elementary school and high school.

A long bout with diphtheria when he was ten
left young Harry with permanently impaired eyesight. He had to wear thick, expensive glasses, which
kept him from participating in many of the games
and sports that other boys enjoyed. He turned in-

stead to reading. By the time he was fourteen he had read every book in the small public library in Independence. His favorite subject was history, which he continued to read about all his life. (Many years after his childhood, he said, "My debt to history is one which cannot be calculated," and he acknowledged that "its lessons were to stand me in good stead . . ." when difficult presidential decisions had to be made.)[1]

During the summers Harry, his sister, Mary Jane, and his younger brother, Vivian, visited their grandparents, the Solomon Youngs, on their farm near Grandview, Missouri. There they helped with the farm chores, rode horseback, and swam in a nearby river. Harry enjoyed farm life, but he wasn't certain he wanted to become a farmer.

Becoming a professional musician was one career that did appeal to young Truman. From the age of thirteen he took piano lessons, first in Independence and later in Kansas City. He loved performing classical numbers, particularly the works of Mozart, Chopin, and Bach. His teachers recognized Harry's talent and urged him to become a concert pianist. Years later he admitted that if he had not gone into politics, he might have tried to earn a living playing the piano.

About the time that Harry graduated from high school, his father suffered severe financial losses, and there was no money for college educations for the children. Harry tried for an appointment to West Point but was turned down because of his poor eyesight. For the next five years he worked at various clerical jobs in or near Kansas City. Then he returned to the family farm near Grandview, where he spent ten years.

If World War I had not occurred, Harry might have continued farming the rest of his life. But he had joined the Missouri National Guard, and when the United States entered the war in 1917, his unit was mobilized as part of the regular army. He took basic training at the Field Artillery School at Fort Sill, Oklahoma, and then was shipped overseas. With the rank of captain, he commanded Battery D of the 129th Field Artillery in battles fought at Mount Herrenberg in the Vosges Mountains and at St. Mihiel. From September to November 1918, Captain Truman's Battery D withstood heavy enemy fire in the important Meuse-Argonne offensive.

After the war ended and Truman came home, he married his childhood sweetheart, Elizabeth Wallace, who was called Bess. They had been classmates from the fifth grade through high school, but their courtship developed slowly, partly because Harry was concerned about earning enough money to support a family. When they married, Harry was thirty-five, Bess was thirty-four. They had one child, Margaret. The family was small but exceptionally close. Although Bess tried to avoid the limelight, even after she became First Lady, her husband affectionately referred to her as his boss and relied heavily on her advice. And he was deeply devoted to his daughter, who, when she reached maturity, pursued a career as a coloratura soprano.

Following his marriage, Truman and an Army friend, Eddie Jacobson, raised some money and opened a haberdashery (men's clothing store) in Kansas City. The success of this business was largely dependent on the economic well-being of the many farmers who lived near Kansas City. During World War I American farmers had been prosperous because of the strong domestic and foreign markets for their products, so at first the clothing store had many customers. But, beginning in 1921, the price of farm products dropped sharply, and soon American farmers were hard hit by a depression. They no longer could afford to buy new clothing, so the haberdashery had to close in 1922. To avoid bankruptcy, Truman faithfully repaid his creditors in installments over the next fifteen years.

While he was serving in the Army, Truman had become a friend of Jim Pendergast, who was the nephew of Tom Pendergast, the heavy-handed Democratic boss of Kansas City. Shortly before the clothing store went out of business, Truman was approached by Mike Pendergast, Tom's brother, and asked to run for the office of judge for the Eastern District of Jackson County. (In Missouri this was an administrative, not a judicial, position, so it did not require a legal background.) Even though Truman previously had not played an active role in politics, the Pendergasts wanted him as their candidate because they had heard he was intelligent, efficient, and a hard worker.

Truman accepted the offer, and, with the powerful support of the Pendergast machine, he won the election. During his two-year term (1922–1924), Truman was industrious and conscientious; he managed to reduce the county debt and at the same time improve county services. In 1924 he was defeated for reelection, but in 1926 he was elected to a higher office, presiding judge of the Jackson County Court. He was reelected in 1930, and during his eight years in office Judge Truman was responsible for spending more than $60 million on highways and building construction. He always insisted on open bidding for construction contracts and careful inspection of all projects financed by taxpayers' money.

The Jackson County judge built a solid reputation for absolute honesty, thrift, and efficiency in contrast to the widely known corruption of the Pendergast machine. In 1934 Boss Pendergast chose him as his candidate for a Senate seat. Truman won the election, but at first Washington reporters reviled him as the puppet of a political machine and called him "the senator from Pendergast." When this graft-ridden machine collapsed and Tom Pendergast was jailed for income tax evasion in 1939, Truman was questioned about his relations with the fallen boss. He acknowledged that the kingpin of Kansas City politics had helped him win elections, but he added emphatically, "Tom Pendergast never asked me to do a dishonest deed. He knew I wouldn't do it if he asked me."[2]

Senator Truman was assigned to the Appropriations and Interstate Commerce committees, and he helped draft some important measures, including the Civil Aeronautics Act to regulate the airline industry. He was a loyal supporter of President Franklin D. Roosevelt and consistently voted in favor of Roosevelt's New Deal programs. But the senator from Missouri felt frustrated in his first term on Capitol Hill. The president considered him one of the Pendergast "boys" and treated him in a distant, aloof manner. Also, Truman found it difficult to make ends meet in expensive Washington, and he had to hire his wife as a secretary to add to the family income.

As the end of his term approached, friends told Truman that with the Pendergast machine in ruins, his chances of reelection were bleak. So he thought seriously of not running for reelection and instead going back to Independence, where life was simpler and he would be surrounded by devoted relatives and friends.

This idea was cast aside, however, when Truman learned that Missouri Governor Lloyd Stark was going to run in the Democratic primary election for his Senate seat, with the blessing of President Roosevelt. In an effort to placate Truman and ease him out of the Senate, Roosevelt offered him an appoint-

140

ment to the Interstate Commerce Commission. This devious gesture enraged Truman, who now was determined to fight for his Senate seat. "I sent the President word," he said afterward, "that I would run if I get only one vote—mine."[3]

The race, he knew, would not be easy. Truman had no money for radio broadcasts, newspaper ads, billboards, or rallies. So he drove around the state in his own car and went to see the people where they lived and worked. Some days he spent fifteen hours popping into farmers' fields and barns, into village stores, restaurants, banks, and courthouses, shaking strangers' hands and asking for their votes.

A few Senate colleagues came into Missouri and gave speeches for Truman. Labor unions began collecting money and providing workers for his campaign. When the votes of the primary election were counted, Truman defeated Stark by a mere 7,476 votes. In the general election the battler from Independence beat his Republican opponent by a more comfortable margin of almost 50,000 votes.

During this 1940 senatorial campaign, Truman had become aware of the waste and inefficiency that existed at munitions factories and Army bases he had visited. The United States was then in the midst of arming for possible entry into World War II, and the Missouri senator wondered whether the misuse of funds for military programs that he had observed in his own state would be found in other states. He toured twelve states in his own car at his own expense to learn how widespread the problem was. The irregularities he saw during his 30,000-mile tour led him to ask the Senate to establish the Committee to Investigate the National Defense Program.

Senator Truman was chairman of this committee, which acquired great importance after the bombing of Pearl Harbor drew the United States into the war. The committee investigated many companies that manufactured or assembled armaments and brought to light numerous cases of waste and mismanagement. It was estimated that by 1944 the work of the committee had saved the government several billion dollars. Later, when fifty news reporters and columnists voted on the ten persons who had made the greatest contributions to the war effort, Truman was the only senator included on the list.

Largely due to the success of this committee, Truman became one of the most respected leaders in the Senate. And President Roosevelt no longer snubbed the man from Missouri who had, after all, helped to save the government an enormous amount of money.

In 1944 when Roosevelt announced that he would seek a fourth term in the White House, political observers were eager to learn who would be his running mate. The president looked weary and gaunt, and widespread rumors suggested that his health was failing. So the 1944 Democratic vice presidential candidate had a good chance of becoming president sometime during the next four years.

John Nance Garner of Texas had been the vice president during Roosevelt's first two terms. But he opposed some New Deal measures and FDR's bid for an unprecedented third term, so Garner stepped down at the end of his second term. Henry Wallace of Iowa was vice president while Roosevelt served his third term. Wallace, however, was much too liberal, erratic, and unpredictable for conservative and moderate Democrats, especially in the South. Fearful that he would carry FDR down to defeat, many party leaders were anxious to have Wallace dropped from the ticket.

On the other hand, Wallace had strong backing from the heads of labor unions and civil rights activ-

142

ists. Roosevelt liked Wallace, but he was shrewd enough to realize that his controversial vice president could lose him many votes. He wrote the chairman of the Democratic convention, explaining that if he were a delegate he personally would vote for Wallace's renomination, but he was willing to let the convention decide who would be his running mate.

The vice presidential candidate whom Truman said he would support was James F. Byrnes of South Carolina, who had compiled a distinguished record as a senator, Supreme Court justice, and director of the Office of War Mobilization. Byrnes asked Truman to give the speech nominating him at the convention, and the Missouri senator agreed. But there was serious opposition to Byrnes in some Democratic circles. His conservatism was not approved of by union leaders; his southern background and views on racial issues antagonized civil rights groups; he had been born a Catholic but renounced that faith, which could cost the Democrats many Catholic votes.

While the convention delegates argued about whether liberal Wallace or conservative Byrnes should be given second place on the ticket, Democratic National Chairman Robert E. Hannegan of Missouri suggested that a deadlock could be averted by selecting his friend and fellow Missourian Harry Truman as a compromise candidate. Truman heard the rumors of his possible nomination when he arrived in Chicago for the convention, but he brushed them aside, declaring that he still supported Byrnes for the job. Hannegan persisted, however, and he wangled from Roosevelt a note saying:

You have written me about Harry Truman and [Supreme Court Justice] Bill Douglas. I should, of course, be very glad to run with either of

them and believe that either one of them would
bring real strength to the ticket.[4]

Hannegan made FDR's note public, but the stubborn senator from Missouri still disclaimed any personal interest in the vice presidency. Finally, Roosevelt himself interceded with a phone call placed to Hannegan while Truman was in the same room. "Have you got that fellow lined up yet?" FDR asked. "No," said Hannegan, "he is the contrariest Missouri mule I've ever dealt with." "Well," replied FDR, "you tell him, if he wants to break up the Democratic party in the middle of the war, that's his responsibility."

Hannegan put down the phone and relayed the president's message to Truman. "Now what do you say?" Hannegan asked. "Well, if that's the situation," Truman snorted, "I'll have to say yes, but why in the hell didn't he tell me in the first place?"[5]

The names of twelve candidates, mostly favorite sons, were placed in nomination for the vice presidency. The first ballot gave Wallace 429½ votes and Truman second place with 319½ votes (Byrnes had dropped out of the race). Truman passed Wallace on the second ballot, and before the results could be announced, enough states switched their votes to Truman to put him over the top. The reluctant candidate soon came to be called "the new Missouri Compromise."

Against the Roosevelt-Truman ticket, the Republicans ran Governor Thomas E. Dewey of New York for president and Governor John W. Bricker of Ohio for vice president. The race was closer than any of FDR's three previous presidential elections, but the Democratic candidates still had a comfortable plurality of more than 3.5 million popular votes, and 432 electoral votes to the Republicans' 99.

FDR served less than three months of his fourth

144

term; on April 12, 1945, he died suddenly from a cerebral hemorrhage. The president's wife, Eleanor Roosevelt, summoned Truman to the White House and told him of her husband's death. Stunned by the sad news, the vice president felt great sympathy for Mrs. Roosevelt and asked if there was anything he could do for her. "Is there anything *we* can do for *you?*" she replied earnestly. "For you are the one in trouble now."[6]

The contrasts between Roosevelt and his successor in the presidency were numerous and significant. Often called "the squire of Hyde Park," FDR came from a socially elite, wealthy family that provided him with a Harvard education and all the material comforts he desired. Truman came from an ordinary farm family that didn't have enough money to send him to college. (He was the only twentieth-century president without a college education.) Roosevelt was an imposing world figure, the dominant leader of the free world at the time of his death; Truman was scarcely known outside Missouri and Washington, D.C. Charismatic FDR had a commanding, self-assured presence (even in a wheelchair) and enormous personal charm. Truman was an ordinary-looking man of average height and weight who wore steel-rimmed glasses, had a hot temper, and frequently offended people by his profane remarks and his willingness to fight in a no-holds-barred style for friends and causes that he wanted to defend.

Even in their ways of speaking, Roosevelt and Truman were distinctly different. Gracious FDR had a dramatic, commanding voice and the capacity to sound like a caring neighbor when he delivered on radio his famous fireside chats to millions of devoted followers. Down-to-earth Truman spoke abruptly in a quick, choppy manner and with an unpleasant nasal twang.

Shortly after Truman assumed the presidency, tremendously important decisions with far-reaching consequences had to be made, but Roosevelt had done nothing to prepare his possible successor for dealing with these matters. Since his inauguration as vice president in January, Truman had seen the president privately only three times, and each visit had been brief and insignificant. On the evening when he was sworn in as the new chief executive, Truman knew nothing about the top-secret atomic bomb, then being developed, and two weeks passed before he was given a complete briefing on its astounding destructive power and its potential use by the military forces.

While World War II was still being fought, the groundwork had been laid for forming a new world organization to prevent future wars. A meeting of representatives from fifty nations was scheduled to begin in San Francisco on April 15—three days after Roosevelt's death. Its purpose was to draft the charter of the United Nations Organization. Even though the free world was still mourning the loss of its beloved leader, President Truman declared that this meeting should begin as planned, and later he journeyed to San Francisco to address its delegates.

The war in Europe ended when Germany accepted terms of unconditional surrender on May 7, 1945, but the United States and Great Britain still had to subdue stubborn Japan. Although American forces had driven the Japanese from many of the islands they had occupied in the Pacific and damaged enemy cities with bombing raids, it appeared that a full-scale invasion of the Japanese mainland might be necessary to bring this Asian country to its knees. Truman's military advisers told the president that such an invasion could prolong the war for at least another year and cause as many as 1 million

American and British casualties before victory could be achieved.

The only apparent alternative to landing huge forces on Japanese soil was to unleash the atomic bomb on carefully selected targets in Japan. But this awesome bomb, with its destructive power equal to 20,000 tons of TNT, could cause a staggering number of civilian casualties. President Truman warned Japan to surrender or face huge losses from a new weapon that was much more devastating than anything the world had ever seen before; millions of leaflets were dropped from planes on Japanese cities, urging the people to demand that their emperor heed Truman's warning. But the Japanese government rejected this ultimatum, and the American president then ordered the first wartime use of atomic power.

An A-bomb was dropped on the city of Hiroshima on August 6, 1945, instantly killing about 80,000 people and mortally wounding at least another 90,000, who died later from radioactivity. A second A-bomb landed on Nagasaki on August 9, and three days later Japan surrendered. Whether it was morally right to attack Japan with these horrendous weapons has been debated ever since President Truman approved the action as a means of ending World War II quickly and decisively. (In a Media General–Associated Press poll taken in August 1989, six in ten people said they believed Truman had acted correctly.)[7]

When the war abroad ended, Truman's battles with Congress began. To help avoid the runaway inflation that traditionally follows wars, the president issued a "hold-the-line order" that extended wartime controls on prices and wages. But many leaders in Congress, echoing the views of a substantial segment of the American public, argued that since the war was over, the government no longer should keep tight reins on the economy. Over Truman's objections the Office of Price Administration (OPA), the agency that had imposed price controls during the war, was shut down in June 1946. Prices soon skyrocketed, as the president had anticipated.

After the war, laborers demanded higher wages to maintain a decent standard of living. Even before the OPA went out of existence, 900,000 workers in several industries went on strike in 1945, and another million joined them in early 1946. The most serious labor disputes came from the United Mine Workers and railroad unions. Soon after the coal miners struck in April 1946, President Truman asserted that their action was a threat to the national interest. He seized the mines in May and held them until an agreement was reached and the strikers went back to work. Meanwhile, a proposed railroad strike was on the verge of crippling vital transportation links, so the president decided to ask Congress for the power to draft striking workers into the Army and force them to run the trains. Just as Truman was about to address Congress on this subject, the railroad employees and owners settled their differences.

From June 1946 on, the Truman administration faced worsening problems in such critical areas as inflation and rising prices, the shortage of consumer goods, and increasingly strident demands from workers that led many people to wonder whether organized labor had grown too powerful. This general dissatisfaction helped account for the huge Republican gains in the congressional elections in November 1946. For the first time since 1930, when Herbert Hoover was president, both houses of Congress were controlled by Republicans.

The new Eightieth Congress lost no time in curbing the power of labor unions. In 1947, over

President Truman's veto, it passed the Taft-Hartley Act, which upheld a worker's right not to be forced to join a union. The Taft-Hartley Act also enabled the attorney general to obtain an injunction (court order) barring for eighty days any strike affecting the national health or safety, and it prohibited unions from contributing to political campaigns.

The Truman administration also faced serious problems in foreign affairs. During World War II the United States, Great Britain, and the Soviet Union were joined in a so-called Grand Alliance to defeat fascist Germany and Italy. (The Soviets did not enter the struggle against Japan until three months following the surrender of Germany, which was after the atomic bomb was dropped on Hiroshima.) At wartime conferences of the Allied leaders, the Soviets had promised that shortly after the conquest of Germany they would permit free elections and independent governments in the Eastern European countries they liberated from Nazi rule.

The Soviets, however, did not keep their promises. Instead, they denied free elections in the countries they occupied and turned them into puppet states dominated by Communist bosses. Soon the Grand Alliance came apart at the seams, to be replaced by a long "Cold War" between the Soviets and their former allies. An impenetrable "Iron Curtain" separated Communist Eastern Europe from democratic Western Europe.

Early in 1947, the British government secretly informed the United States that it no longer could keep its troops in Greece. These troops had been protecting Greece from a takeover by Communist guerrillas, who were getting military support from behind the Iron Curtain. President Truman believed that if Greece fell to the Communists—which was virtually certain without foreign aid—Turkey would go next, then perhaps the Middle East or Italy. The president decided that the United States must act at once to prevent this domino effect from taking place. He asked Congress for $400 million in military and economic assistance to Greece and Turkey; Congress appropriated the money, and these two countries did not fall under Communist domination.

This help extended to Greece and Turkey, commonly called the Truman Doctrine, was an American answer to Russian ambitions throughout the free world. It gave birth to the policy known as "containment." The essential purpose of containment was to keep communism within its existing boundaries. It told the Soviet Union that it could expand no farther without risking war with the United States.

Meanwhile, the countries of Western Europe had been ravaged by the war and lay prostrate, unable to find the resources to rebuild their economies. There was a growing danger that Communists in some of these countries, especially France and Italy, would gain control of their weak governments. President Truman and Secretary of State George C. Marshall realized that these nations needed substantial financial aid from the United States to revitalize their economic structures. In June 1947 Marshall proposed a plan whereby the United States would help all European countries in a common effort to eradicate poverty by raising production sharply. (Marshall included the Soviet Union and its Iron Curtain satellites in his offer, but the Communist states refused to cooperate.) The Marshall Plan was immensely successful. Between 1948 and 1952 the United States pumped about $13 billion into reconstruction projects that helped Western Europe move from depression and despair to prosperity and confidence.

Following the war, Germany had been divided into two countries: free, democratic West Germany and Communist East Germany. The city of Berlin, which lay 110 miles inside East Germany, also was divided into free West Berlin and Communist East Berlin. In the summer of 1948 the Communists suddenly closed all the highways, railroads, and water routes that ran from West Germany to West Berlin. They believed that when the West Berliners no longer could get food and fuel from West Germany they would be forced to surrender their freedom.

President Truman, however, was determined to prevent West Berlin from falling to the Communists. He ordered the launching of a risky Berlin airlift to supply the needs of a city of 2 million people. Night and day cargo ships flew in food, clothing, medical supplies, and coal to the beleaguered West Berliners. Finally, after the siege had lasted ten months, the Communists reluctantly lifted their blockade.

Despite Truman's accomplishments, he was thought to have almost no chance to win a four-year term as president in 1948. There were many sources of domestic discontent: soaring inflation and the rising cost of living, high taxes, labor strife, and rumors of Communist spies employed in high government positions. Foreign affairs matters also disturbed many voters. Reactionary conservatives charged Truman was "soft" on Communism, pointing to the enormous gains made by the Soviets in Eastern Europe since the end of World War II and to the civil war in China in which the Communists were routing the Nationalist forces under Chiang Kai-shek. Radical liberals, on the other hand, attacked Truman for his "hard" line toward the Communists, which they said antagonized leaders in the Kremlin and raised the specter of a horrible war between the superpowers.

After the Republicans swept the congressional elections in 1946, their fortunes seemed to be on the rise, and virtually all political omens indicated they would regain the White House for the first time since 1933. Truman's popularity, according to the polls, had dropped to a record low. There was serious talk among Democrats of not running him for president in 1948—thus saddling Truman with the same fate that befell four of the six previous accidental presidents, whose own party refused to give them the opportunity to seek a four-year term. Some prominent Democrats approached General Dwight D. Eisenhower and asked him to replace Truman at the head of their ticket, but the popular war hero told them he was not interested in seeking the presidency.

When Eisenhower could not be tempted to enter politics in 1948, the Democrats felt they had no other choice than to nominate Truman as their standard-bearer. An atmosphere of gloom and impending defeat prevailed at the Democratic convention when the president began his acceptance address at two o'clock in the morning. But Truman's fiery speech was so inspiring that the weary, disillusioned delegates were roused to their feet and cheered loudly. The president angrily condemned the Eightieth Congress as a "do-nothing" legislature and dramatically announced that he was calling it into special session to cope with some of the pressing problems it had left unresolved.

In the general election Truman faced serious opposition from *three* political parties: the Republican party and two splinter groups of former Democrats.

The Republican ticket included two popular, moderate governors: Thomas E. Dewey of New York was making his second bid for the presidency, and Earl Warren of California was his running mate.

One of the new parties was formed after thirty-five southern delegates to the Democratic convention walked out when the Democratic party put strong civil rights planks in its platform. The anti-Truman southerners called themselves the States' Rights party, held their own convention, which was attended by delegates from thirteen states, and chose South Carolina Governor J. Strom Thurmond as their presidential nominee.

The fourth political party was composed of some liberal Democrats as well as more radical individuals, including some Communists. Officially named the new Progressive party, it ran Henry Wallace for the presidency. Its platform denounced what it called "anti-Soviet hysteria" and demanded that the United States adopt a friendlier, gentler attitude toward the Communist countries.

Truman, not discouraged by the huge odds against him, embarked on a strenuous "whistle-stop" railroad campaign that covered 31,000 miles and lasted two months. The battler from Missouri delivered more than 300 speeches to about 6 million listeners. Whether he spoke to a handful of voters from the observation car of his train or addressed a large rally, the spunky president kept hammering away at the Republican Eightieth Congress, blaming it for being insensitive to the needs of ordinary citizens. "Give 'em hell, Harry!" shouted a man at a Seattle rally. Truman jauntily responded that he just told the truth and the opposition thought it was hell.

Even though the crowds that heard the chief executive warmly applauded his remarks, on Election Eve hardly anyone except Truman himself believed he could finish first in a race against an attractive Republican ticket and two splinter groups of former Democrats who had deserted their party. Yet the underdog president achieved the most astonishing upset in the history of presidential elections. He amassed 303 electoral votes to 189 for Dewey, 39 for Thurmond, and none for Wallace. While Truman did not quite win half of the popular vote, he led Dewey by more than 2 million votes and held both Thurmond and Wallace to a little over 1 million votes apiece.

The Democrats also regained control of Congress in the 1948 elections. A short time later, President Truman urged Congress to adopt his program of liberal domestic measures, commonly called the "Fair Deal," which was a continuation and expansion of FDR's New Deal. Congress acted favorably on some provisions of the Fair Deal and rejected others. It passed the Housing Act of 1949, which appropriated federal funds for slum clearance and urban renewal. It also broadened Social Security coverage and increased the minimum wage. But Congress turned down some of the president's major proposals: it refused to repeal the Taft-Hartley Act, or pass a federal anti-poll-tax bill, or establish a system of national health insurance for older citizens.

In April 1949 the United States reversed its traditional policy of having no permanent foreign alliances. With President Truman's unequivocal support the United States and nine European countries, plus Canada and Iceland, formed a military alliance called the North Atlantic Treaty Organization (NATO). By the NATO agreement, each country was committed to treat an attack on any one of them as an attack on all the member countries. The Senate ratified the NATO treaty, and the United States sent troops and arms to NATO's various European bases. General Eisenhower became the first commander of NATO.

Also in 1949 President Truman unveiled his "Point Four" plan, which marked the beginning of the United States' policy to provide assistance to Third World countries. The plan called for sending American funds and technical aid to underdeveloped lands in the hope that this would encourage them to help

154

themselves. This farsighted program brought badly needed assistance to many impoverished countries, mainly in Latin America, Africa, and Asia.

The peninsula of Korea was an area of increasing concern to the Truman administration. At the end of World War II, Korea, like Germany, had been divided into two countries. Non-Communists controlled South Korea; a Communist government, strongly backed by the Soviet Union and China, was set up in North Korea.

In June 1950, troops from North Korea invaded South Korea. Within hours after the attack, President Truman sent American ships and planes to help South Korea. The Security Council of the United Nations hastily assembled and declared that the invasion constituted an unwarranted act of armed aggression; it voted that the United Nations would come to the defense of South Korea. (The Soviet Union was not able to veto this resolution because at that time it was boycotting UN sessions.)

The UN forces, commanded by America's General Douglas MacArthur, consisted mainly of Americans and South Koreans. They launched a counter-offensive in the fall of 1950 that drove the invaders back into their own land. Then General MacArthur ordered his troops to pursue the enemy into North Korea. When the UN forces pushed so far north that they neared the Yalu River, which separated North Korea from China, the war took an ominous new turn. Hundreds of thousands of Chinese Communist "volunteers" poured into North Korea and drove the UN army southward.

General MacArthur now called for an all-out war against China. President Truman, fearful that extending the conflict could set off World War III, insisted on restricting the fighting to Korea. When MacArthur persisted in publicly rebuking his commander in chief, the president relieved the general of his duty in Korea and replaced him with General Matthew Ridgway.

MacArthur immediately returned home to a hero's welcome, and some of his outspoken supporters demanded that Truman be impeached. But the president firmly held his ground, reminding the public that military power is subject to civilian rule in the United States. He defended his dismissal of MacArthur as an appropriate response to a general who was willing to risk turning a limited war into a worldwide atomic conflagration. (The Korean War dragged on past the end of the Truman presidency. It finally ended in 1953, and the peace settlement established a North Korea–South Korea boundary which was almost the same as the border that had existed between these two countries before the war began.)

The Cold War and the Korean War caused many Americans to fear that Communists were operating within this country and, quite possibly, within the national government. President Truman authorized a sweeping investigation into the backgrounds and beliefs of all federal employees. Before he left office, loyalty checks had been run on over 6 million people. A few hundred were dismissed as possible loyalty risks; another few thousand resigned.

This action, however, failed to stem the growing "Red Scare." In 1950 Congress passed, over President Truman's veto, a tough Internal Security Act. It required all Communists to register with the Justice Department, permitted the deportation of any alien who had ever been a Communist, and forbade employment of Communists in jobs related to national defense. The president vetoed this measure because he felt it could become the basis for unconstitutional violations of civil rights.

Sensational spy trials fueled the Red Scare that gripped the country. The anti-Communist hysteria reached its height when Wisconsin Senator Joseph McCarthy asserted in February 1950 that he had a list of 205 known Communists working in the State Department, and that this proved that the Roosevelt and Truman administrations had indulged in "twenty years of treason." When he was pressed to reveal the names of these "traitors," McCarthy was unable to provide a single one. But even though he failed to produce a single shred of evidence to substantiate this wild charge, in the atmosphere of the time the senator gained an ever-increasing following. President Truman, however, refused to be bullied by the Wisconsin senator and considered him a vicious liar.

Truman never dodged a fight when he felt that his cause was just, but, like some other strong presidents, occasionally he overstepped his authority. One example of this was when, in April 1952, he ordered the federal government to seize steel mills to prevent an impending strike. The steel mill owners filed a lawsuit against the government, and the Supreme Court ruled in their favor, declaring that the president had exceeded his constitutional powers.

After Truman left the presidency in 1953, he returned to his home in Independence, Missouri. He continued an active interest in world affairs and campaigned for Democratic candidates. In 1965, when the former president was eighty-one years old, President Lyndon B. Johnson traveled to Independence to sign into law the Medicare Act that Truman had proposed to Congress sixteen years earlier.

Truman died in 1972 at the age of eighty-eight. He was buried in Independence, in the courtyard behind the Truman Library, which he had founded. His wife, Bess, died ten years later at the age of ninety-seven; she had the longest life of any First Lady.

Harry Truman was an outspoken man whose bursts of profanity and displays of temper sometimes were criticized as demeaning the dignity of his high office. His critics have attacked him for some of the critical decisions he made—trying to continue wartime economic controls after hostilities ceased, promoting social reforms that had to be financed by taxpayers, starting the "containment" policy that led to the United States' assuming the role of a policeman protecting the entire free world, limiting the scope of the Korean War and dismissing General MacArthur. And there are those who still blame President Truman for the most fateful of all the decisions he made: unleashing atomic bombs on civilian populations.

Nevertheless, the president achieved notable successes at a time when momentous events were happening across the world stage at a breathtaking pace. Truman brought the United States into the United Nations, something that President Woodrow Wilson had failed to accomplish in a similar situation when the League of Nations was created. President Truman successfully countered the Soviet Union at every stage of the Cold War: he prevented the imminent fall of Greece and Turkey, bolstered Western Europe with the Marshall Plan, called the Communists' bluff with the Berlin airlift, offered assistance to Third World countries whose underdevelopment made them prey to Communist infiltration, and forged a strong NATO military alliance against potential aggressors. When the Korean War broke out, Truman quickly dispatched U.S. forces to thwart the Communists' attempt to seize South Korea. And by firing an insubordinate General MacArthur, Truman demonstrated that civilian rule must take precedence over military control in a democracy.

On the domestic front, Truman met with only

partial success in coaxing his Fair Deal proposals through Congress. But nearly all of the measures that the legislature rejected during his presidency, such as Medicare, have since been enacted into law.

Harry Truman proved that a plain man without the advantages of wealth, social position, or an extensive formal education could become a successful president if he were honest, decisive, and courageous. The man from Missouri never shirked any responsibility that was relevant to his presidency; the plaque on his desk that read "The buck stops here" summed up the way he felt about the most awesome job in the free world.

Chapter 9
Lyndon B. Johnson:
Civil Rights President

"A United States senator was born today—my grandson!"[1] This proud message was gladly proclaimed by Sam Johnson, Sr., as he rode his horse from farmhouse to farmhouse, sharing the good news with all his neighbors. Old Sam felt certain that Lyndon Baines Johnson, his grandson born on August 27, 1908, was destined to have a brilliant political career.

Lyndon was the first of five children—two sons and three daughters—born to Rebekah and Sam Johnson, Jr. At the time of Lyndon's birth, his parents lived in a three-room farmhouse on the Pedernales River in central Texas. After their third child was born, the Johnsons moved to a larger house in a nearby town called Johnson City. (The town was named after its founder, James K. Johnson, a nephew of Sam, Sr.)

For a long time, politics had played an important role in the activities of the Johnson family. One of Lyndon's ancestors had been governor of Tennessee, and Lyndon's maternal grandfather had served Texas as its secretary of state and later as a representative in the state legislature. Lyndon's father had held various jobs, including rancher, cotton trader, schoolteacher, real estate salesman, and railroad inspector, but his greatest desire was to hold a political office. Sam Johnson, Jr., reached this goal when he was elected to the Texas House of Representatives in 1905. He served in the state legislature until 1909 and again from 1917 to 1925.

As a young boy, Lyndon's favorite pastime was listening to his father discuss politics with the friends and relatives who visited their home. When he was older he helped his father campaign for office and occasionally sat in the gallery of the state legislature, keenly following every word of the debates on the floor. Young Lyndon was eager to become a politician too, and he set his sights on ascending to the top of the ladder, confiding to a classmate that "someday I'm going to be president of the United States."[2]

Lyndon attended the local schools, but he disliked studying and did not work hard in his classes. On the other hand, he excelled in all areas of leadership. In high school he was senior-class president and a member of the school debating team that won some regional meets. To earn some pocket money, he shined shoes in Johnson City's only barber shop and herded goats for the ranchers.

When Lyndon graduated from high school in 1924, his mother wanted him to go to college. But the tall, lanky youth, who was not quite sixteen, was not ready for the rigors of higher education. Instead, with four other teenagers, he set out for California in a Model T Ford. The other boys found employment in a cement factory at Tehachapi or worked at odd jobs. Lyndon lived with a lawyer cousin in San

Bernardino and served as a clerk in his law office. In addition, he took a part-time job as an elevator operator in the same building.

About a year later, homesick and nearly penniless, Lyndon returned to Johnson City. He was hired to do menial labor with a road-building crew; Lyndon drove open trucks and scooped up the dirt where roads would be laid. It was hard, dirty work, but the young Texan stuck to the job for about sixteen months. His mother kept pleading with him to start college, and finally he agreed to enroll at Southwest Texas State Teachers College in San Marcos. "I'd just gone through January on the road gang," Johnson later reminisced, "and it was cold weather, very cold. At that moment the prospect of going to school in the spring had some appeal to me. I said I'd do it."[3]

Lyndon hitchhiked to the San Marcos campus and began his studies to become a teacher. He earned high grades in political science, history, and education courses, but did less well in mathematics and science. He was on the debating team, wrote articles for the college newspaper, and took an active part in school politics, including membership on the student council. His father had suffered financial losses, so Lyndon had to work his way through college. At first he was a school janitor, but later he became a secretary to the college president.

Forced to drop out of school temporarily when his money ran out, Lyndon spent nine months teaching poor Mexican-American children in the small southern Texas town of Cotulla. He won high praise both as a teacher and as a warm friend of the underprivileged youngsters. Lyndon made learning an exciting experience in his classroom and helped secure badly needed athletic equipment for the school playgound. (Many years later his former students in Cotulla established a Lyndon Johnson Alumni Club in honor of their famous teacher.)

162

Lyndon resumed his college work at Texas State Teachers College and received his bachelor's degree in education in August 1930. In the fall of that year, young Mr. Johnson began teaching speech and debate at Sam Houston High School in Houston. He enjoyed working with students, but when the opportunity came to take a political job in the nation's capital, he could not resist the offer.

Johnson had campaigned in 1931 for the election of Richard M. Kleberg, a wealthy Democrat, to the House of Representatives. When Kleberg won, Johnson went with him to Washington, where he served for four years as Kleberg's secretary. The former schoolteacher quickly learned all the duties of his new position, and he made friends easily. He soon acquired a reputation as one of the hardest workers and most skillful politicians on Capitol Hill. His coworkers recognized Johnson's exceptional talents by electing him speaker of the "Little Congress," an organization of congressional secretaries.

In 1934 Johnson met Claudia Alta (Lady Bird) Taylor, the daughter of a prosperous Texas rancher, and he knew immediately that she was the woman he wanted to marry. (Lady Bird had acquired her nickname as a baby when a family servant said she was as pretty "as a ladybird.") Lyndon proposed marriage the day after he was introduced to Lady Bird, who was only twenty-one and had just graduated from the University of Texas. She was leery of rushing into marriage, but her determined suitor, applying the same zeal and persistence that he demonstrated in his political career, flooded her with love letters. Lady Bird finally consented, and they were married on November 17, 1934, at St Mark's Episcopal Church in San Antonio, Texas.

The Johnsons had two daughters—Lynda Bird, born in 1944, and Luci Baines, born in 1947. (In 1967 Lynda Bird married Marine Captain Charles S.

Robb, who became governor of Virginia in 1981 and was elected to the United States Senate in 1988.)

Mrs. Johnson was an astute businesswoman who acquired wealth for the family while her husband was in public office. She spent part of an inheritance from her father to gain control of a small radio station in Texas that was losing money. When it prospered under her direction, she invested in other radio and television stations and purchased large real estate properties.

While Johnson was working as a congressional secretary, Franklin D. Roosevelt was elected president, and his New Deal was launched to combat the severe economic hardships caused by the Great Depression. The National Youth Administration (NYA) was one of the New Deal agencies established to help needy young people. In 1935, upon the recommendation of Congressman Sam Rayburn, one of his father's political friends, Johnson was appointed director of the NYA for the state of Texas.

The NYA was designed to keep youths in school or, if they were not attending school, to find them jobs. Johnson applied his extraordinary organizational ability to securing either part-time or full-time employment for tens of thousands of young Texans. Many of them helped to construct roadside parks, schools, and libraries. Others learned new trades through extensive training programs. Johnson's NYA operation soon became a model for the nation, and even First Lady Eleanor Roosevelt went to Texas to see firsthand the remarkable job that its energetic, efficient director was doing.

When the congressional seat in Johnson's Tenth District fell vacant in 1937 following the death of Representative James P. Buchanan, a special election was held to fill this office. Johnson decided to enter the contest. There were nine candidates in the field, and several of the others were better known and more experienced than the twenty-eight-year-old NYA director. Lyndon clearly needed some characteristic that would distinguish him from the other eight contenders. So he campaigned on the platform that he was the only candidate who supported all of President Roosevelt's policies; this included FDR's controversial attempt to expand the Supreme Court from nine to fifteen members in order to add new justices who would endorse his New Deal measures.

Johnson's strategy succeeded and, although he won only 27 percent of the votes cast, he led the other candidates and was elected to the House of Representatives. Word of Johnson's loyalty reached the White House, and a short time later when the president ended a fishing trip in Texas, he asked to see the new congressman. FDR then invited Johnson to ride with him on the presidential train from Galveston to Forth Worth, 315 miles away. The two men enjoyed each other's company, and Johnson expressed a strong interest in the Navy, which greatly pleased the president. Soon after Johnson took his seat in Congress, FDR arranged for him to become a member of the powerful House Naval Affairs Committee.

Congressman Johnson worked diligently for his home district. He obtained millions of government dollars for local projects, and he was instrumental in bringing electrification by public, rather than expensive private, power companies to thousands of homes in rural areas. He was reelected to the House five times, sometimes without opposition.

In 1941 one of the senators from Texas died, and Johnson entered the special election for the vacant office. His chief opponent was popular Governor W. Lee O'Daniel. Johnson ran a strong race, but he lost to O'Daniel by the narrow margin of 1,311 votes. After this defeat, Johnson took a more conservative stance. He supported more forcefully the powerful Texas oil interests, and he opposed civil rights measures, which were unpopular in his southwestern state. Johnson claimed he was not prejudiced toward blacks, but in the 1940s and early 1950s he maintained that issues pertaining to civil rights should be resolved by individual states, not the national government.

The day following the Japanese attack on Pearl Harbor, Johnson became the first member of Congress to enter active duty in World War II. A lieutenant commander in the Navy, he was stationed in the South Pacific. In June 1942 he was on a B-26 bomber headed for a Japanese base when one engine failed and the crippled plane became an easy target for enemy fire. The B-26 was hit several times, but somehow it limped back to the American headquarters at Port Moresby, New Guinea. Johnson was awarded the Silver Star for "gallant action." Later that same year he returned to Washington when President Roosevelt ordered that all congressmen in the armed forces resume their legislative duties.

After the war Johnson made his second bid for a Senate seat. The year was 1948, and at that time winning the Democratic primary election in Texas virtually assured the candidate victory in the general election because the state's Republican party was then small and weak. Former Governor Coke Stevenson was favored to win the Democratic nomination, and he defeated Johnson and nine other candidates in the first stage of the primary election. But Stevenson failed to win a majority of votes, so a runoff election was scheduled between him and runner-up Johnson.

Since he had to give up his House seat to run for the Senate, Johnson knew that his political career might be ended if he lost the election. He campaigned strenuously from dawn until late at night and even hired a helicopter to whisk him from one rally to another. The election was a cliffhanger: the State Democratic Executive Committee certified that Johnson won by only 87 votes out of nearly 1 million votes cast.

Stevenson challenged the results, claiming fraud in three south Texas counties. Both sides uncovered many irregularities, such as destroyed ballots, errors in the vote counts, and the names of dead people on voting rolls. Stevenson's charges were upheld, but this ruling was overturned by Supreme Court Justice Hugo Black. Even the United States Senate investigated the election, deciding there was no clear proof of fraud but many charges of such on both sides.[4] Johnson, who meanwhile had decisively beaten his Republican opponent in the general election, was allowed to take his seat in the Senate. But the closeness of his controversial victory at the polls earned him the sarcastic nickname of "Landslide Lyndon."

Even though his first term began under a cloud of suspicion, Johnson became one of the most able and effective legislators in the history of the Senate. He served on the Senate Armed Forces Committee, where he advocated strong military preparedness as the best deterrent to Communist expansion. He headed the Senate Preparedness Investigating Subcommittee, which uncovered instances of military inefficiency and waste during the Korean War. An early supporter of the nation's space program, he was the first chairman of the Senate Aeronautics and Space Sciences Committee. He worked for the passage of bills increasing the minimum wage and extending Social Security benefits.

Democratic colleagues in the Senate recognized Johnson's leadership qualities by naming him party whip in 1951. Two years later they elected him minority leader of the Senate. At that time Republican Dwight D. Eisenhower was president and his party narrowly controlled the Senate. But in the next congressional election the Democrats recaptured the Senate, and Johnson became majority leader in 1955, at the age of forty-six. Never had a senator risen so quickly to such high leadership positions.

Democrat Johnson refused to oppose the Republican in the White House just because he and Eisenhower belonged to different political parties. Instead, he pursued a policy of conciliation and compromise, which was in accord with a maxim from the prophet Isaiah that he often quoted: "Come now, and let us reason together."[5] Johnson helped steer through the Senate such Eisenhower proposals as the Formosa Resolution warning Communist China not to invade what is now Taiwan, the Mutual Security Act, the Reciprocal Trade Agreement, and a minimum-wage reform bill.

The majority leader's powers of persuasion were both astounding and relentless. A physically impressive man who stood 6 feet 3 inches tall and weighed about 210 pounds, Johnson would heartily shake a colleague's hand and embrace his shoulders with a mighty bear hug. To secure needed votes for a measure, he would coax, cajole, flatter, tease, and sometimes admonish fellow senators. His energy seemed boundless, and it was common for him to work fifteen hours a day. But Johnson achieved outstanding results. Time and time again the Senate passed controversial measures he supported, and the majority leader, whom reporters often called "LBJ," became the most powerful figure, next to the president, in the national government.

Johnson's strenuous life-style may have contributed to the onset of a moderately severe heart attack in 1955. This forced him to the sidelines temporarily, but after several months of recuperation the majority leader returned to the Senate floor.

A remarkable change occurred in Johnson's political philosophy in the late 1950s. Before that time he had consistently voted with southern legislators against civil rights bills. But he did a complete about-face in 1957 and, riding herd over protesting southern colleagues, LBJ shepherded through the Senate the first civil rights bill since 1875. Later, Johnson led the successful battle for the Civil Rights Act of 1960. Both the 1957 and 1960 measures provided limited benefits for minorities, but they foretold the direction LBJ would take in subsequent years.

Johnson aspired to be elected president in 1960, but he did not wage an active campaign in the state primary elections to help select the Democratic nominee. Instead, he tended to Senate business and waited until five days before the Democratic convention opened to announce that he was a serious candidate. By that time John F. Kennedy, the youthful, charismatic Massachusetts senator, had virtually locked up the nomination. When the delegates cast their votes on the first ballot, Kennedy was nominated with 806 votes and Johnson finished second with 409 votes.

Then followed the most startling development at the 1960 Democratic convention. Most delegates were surprised when Kennedy asked Johnson to be his running mate; they were dumbfounded when LBJ agreed to accept the vice presidential nomination. If the Kennedy-Johnson ticket were to win, the Senate majority leader would have to give up the enormous power he then held in order to assume a much weaker and less conspicuous government office. (Texas law permitted Johnson to run for vice president and re-election to the Senate at the same time, so his seat in Congress seemed secure if he lost his race for the vice presidency.)

For the next four months, Johnson campaigned enthusiastically for the Democratic ticket. He traveled through the South and Southwest on an eleven-car train that covered about 3,500 miles. The "LBJ Victory Special" stopped at nearly every crossroads, and the tall, hefty Texan would emerge to remind the crowds of his party's accomplishments and goals, and to condemn the policies advanced by the Republican presidential nominee, Vice President Richard Nixon.

Johnson's role in the campaign proved to be significant, perhaps even critical, in helping Kennedy defeat Nixon by a razor-thin margin. The two presidential candidates almost tied in the popular vote, but Kennedy won 303 electoral votes to Nixon's 219. However, Kennedy's total electoral votes included 56 from the states of Texas, Louisiana, North Carolina, and South Carolina—all states in which the candidacy of LBJ may have largely accounted for the Democratic triumph.

President Kennedy lived up to a campaign promise to make his vice president an active partner in the executive branch of the government. Johnson attended sessions of the cabinet and the National Security Council, conferred privately with Kennedy, and served as the president's liaison with Congress. He headed the President's Committee on Equal Employment Opportunity, which attempted to end racial discrimination in the hiring practices of government contractors. Also, after Kennedy launched the Peace Corps to provide American help to people in underdeveloped countries, Johnson chaired the Peace Corps Advisory Council.

LBJ represented the president on goodwill tours to more than thirty nations. Secret Service agents assigned to guard him were shocked when the vice president plunged into crowds to shake outstretched hands, but Johnson was determined to meet the ordinary people wherever he traveled. On one trip he met a Pakistani camel driver and invited him to come to his LBJ Ranch in Texas. The camel driver accepted the invitation, and his visit to the vice president's ranch on the Pedernales River was a highly publicized event.

On the fateful day of November 22, 1963, Johnson and his wife were riding two cars behind the president's car in a procession through downtown Dallas. When President Kennedy was shot, an alert Secret Service agent, fearful of other attacks, pushed the vice president below the car windows. As soon as he learned that the president had died, Johnson decided to return immediately to Washington. Aboard *Air Force One* at the Dallas airport, Johnson was administered the presidential oath by Sarah T. Hughes, a federal judge.

A stunned and saddened nation looked to the new president for strength and reassurance. In a nationally televised address to Congress shortly after Kennedy's funeral, Johnson said that Americans could best honor the slain president's memory and vision by moving ahead in the direction that Kennedy had charted in his administration. "Let us continue," declared the new president softly and solemnly; this was a deliberate response to Kennedy's famous challenge "Let us begin."[6]

In January 1964 Johnson started his crusade for reform legislation. During one congressional session at least twenty important bills were passed, including a substantial tax cut that helped ensure a growing economy. One major legislative achievement was the Economic Opportunity Act of 1964, which funded various antipoverty programs. Among these programs were (1) VISTA, a domestic Peace Corps, (2) the Job Corps, to provide vocational training to poor

171

youth, (3) Head Start, to help disadvantaged preschoolers become ready for the classroom, (4) the Work-Study Program, which provided part-time jobs for needy college students, and (5) the Work Experience Program, which brought child day care to poverty-stricken families and freed mothers to work.

Other bills signed by the new president authorized almost $3 billion for aid to education and more than $1.5 billion for public works. But the most significant measure passed by Congress in Johnson's first year in office was the Civil Rights Act of 1964.

This bill had been introduced in Congress in July 1963, following nationwide civil rights demonstrations, but President Kennedy had been unable to muster enough votes for its passage. Johnson, as president, brought his consummate persuasive powers to bear on Congress, and this historic law was enacted. Its provisions outlawed discrimination in public accommodations (such as hotels, restaurants, and other facilities open to the public), set up an Equal Opportunity Commission to end employment discrimination, authorized the Department of Justice to file lawsuits to facilitate school integration, forbade segregation in federally funded projects, and provided improved voting safeguards. Ironically, the White House was not occupied by a northerner when this—the most sweeping civil rights bill in the nation's history—became the law of the land.

Johnson called his domestic program the "Great Society." In a commencement speech at the University of Michigan in May 1964, he declared:

We have the opportunity to move not only toward the rich society and the powerful society, but upward to the Great Society. The Great Society rests on abundance and liberty for all. It demands an end to poverty and racial injustice. . . . The Great Society is a place where every

172

child can find knowledge to enrich his mind and to enlarge his talents. . . . It is a place where the city of man serves not only the needs of the body and the demands of commerce but the desire for beauty and the hunger for community.[7]

The audience listened with rapt attention as the president summoned all Americans to improve and enhance their society. "Let us from this moment begin our work," he concluded, "so that in the future men will look back and say: It was then, after a long and weary way, that man turned the exploits of his genius to the full enrichment of his life."[8]

The 1964 Democratic convention was held in Atlantic City, New Jersey. At that time President Johnson was so popular with his party that he was nominated by acclamation for a four-year term. He appeared before the convention to announce that Senator Hubert Humphrey of Minnesota was his choice for the vice presidential nomination, and the delegates honored his request.

For president the Republicans nominated an ultraconservative candidate, Senator Barry Goldwater of Arizona. Many political observers considered Goldwater a right-wing extremist. The Arizona senator seemed to fit this description, because in his acceptance speech he declared: "I would remind you that extremism in the defense of liberty is no vice. And let me remind you also that moderation in the pursuit of justice is no virtue."[9]

Goldwater's warlike attitude toward the role of the United States in the Vietnam War frightened many voters. During the administration of President Kennedy, American participation in the Vietnam War had been limited and minimal. But as the war dragged on, Goldwater suggested that American field commanders might use nuclear weapons to fight the

Communists in Vietnam. "When you say 'nuclear,' all the American people see is a mushroom cloud," he asserted. "But for military purposes, it's just enough firepower to get the job done." [10] Also, Goldwater advocated taking the United States out of the United Nations if China were admitted to that world body.

On the domestic front, at various times the Arizona senator proposed that Social Security be made voluntary, that public power projects like TVA be abolished, and that federal aid for education and agricultural subsidies be ended. Goldwater firmly championed states' rights and was one of a few Republican senators who voted against the Civil Rights Act of 1964.

"All the Way with LBJ" was the Democrats' slogan, and when the votes were counted it became apparent that almost the entire country had marched to Johnson's drum. He won a record-shattering 61.05 percent of the popular vote, and 486 electoral votes to 52 for Goldwater. LBJ carried forty-four states, including some states that had seldom voted Democratic, including Vermont, New Hampshire, Kansas, Nebraska, and Utah. (Vermont had never before been won by a Democratic presidential candidate.) Goldwater captured only his home state and five states in the Deep South.

Johnson was at the height of his popularity following his landslide victory over Goldwater, and he interpreted the election results as a clear mandate to push full-steam ahead on his Great Society proposals. In 1965 he flooded Congress with a torrent of major bills, more than any other president had sent to Capitol Hill in one legislative session—even eclipsing the record set by Franklin D. Roosevelt's first year in the White House during the Great Depression. *New York Times* columnist Tom Wicker cried out in astonishment, "They are rolling the bills out of Congress these days the way Detroit turns super-sleek, souped-up autos off the assembly line."[11] By October 1965, when Congress recessed, ninety of the administration's legislative recommendations had been passed by Congress and enacted into law.

Among the new laws were measures providing federal aid to impoverished Appalachia; huge government expenditures for elementary, secondary, and higher education; omnibus housing projects; and the creation of the cabinet-level Department of Housing and Urban Development (HUD). Johnson named as secretary of HUD Robert C. Weaver, the first black member of a president's cabinet. (In 1967 Johnson appointed the first black Supreme Court justice, Thurgood Marshall.)

Ugly events in the town of Selma, Alabama, prompted another important law passed in 1965. The population of Selma was almost evenly divided between blacks and whites, yet the people on its voting rolls were nearly all white. To protest this voting rights form of discrimination, Dr. Martin Luther King, Jr., had organized a march by more than 500 civil rights demonstrators from Selma to the state capital at Montgomery. While preparations were being made for the march, state troopers assaulted the demonstrators and a Unitarian minister died following a beating. After President Johnson federalized the state national guard and sent in additional U.S. troops, the pilgrimage proceeded, with the ranks of the protesters swelling to about 3,200 at the beginning of the march and to about 25,000 when the demonstrators reached Montgomery. But while a woman was driving marchers from Montgomery back to Selma, she was stopped by members of the Ku Klux Klan and murdered.

The tragic injustice at Selma weighed heavily on

President Johnson's mind when he delivered a special address to Congress a short time later. The president began by saying:

At times history and fate meet at a single time in a single place to shape a turning point in man's unending search for freedom. So it was at Lexington and Concord. So it was a century ago at Appomattox. So it was last week in Selma, Alabama.[12]

Johnson then asked Congress for a new law that would enable all blacks to fully exercise their rights at the polls. He ended his message by reminding the nation that what happened at Selma was "part of a far larger movement which reaches into every section and state of America. . . . [The blacks'] cause must be our cause, too. . . . And we shall overcome."[13]

Congress responded a few months later with the Voting Rights Act, which empowered the federal government to suspend all literacy and other tests for voting in areas where less than half of the adults were registered to vote. The act also allowed the national government to send registrars to supervise the enrollment of voters in districts where tests were suspended. This landmark law paved the way for a large increase in the number of black voters. (Later, President Johnson obtained another legislative victory for minorities with the passage of the Civil Rights Act of 1968, which prohibited discrimination in the sale and rental of housing.)

The elderly also were substantially helped by Great Society legislation. In July 1965 LBJ signed into law the Medicare Bill, which provided hospital care for Americans sixty-five years of age or older, through an increase in the Social Security tax. Medicare also

176

included an optional medical insurance plan whereby the elderly enrollees paid low monthly premiums to receive doctors' care. Another health program established by Congress was Medicaid, which provided hospital and medical benefits for poor people of any age.

Environmental protection was still another aspect of Great Society legislation. The Water Quality Act of 1965 required states to draw up water quality standards that had to be approved by the Interior Department. Under the Clean Waters Restoration Act of 1966, action was started to purify the nation's lakes and rivers. The Clean Air Act of 1965 empowered the federal government to set up emission standards for curtailing toxic pollutants caused by automobiles. This was followed by the Air Quality Act of 1967, appropriating more than $428 million to fight air pollution. When President Johnson signed this bill, he warned that "either we stop poisoning our air or we become a nation of gas masks, groping our way through the dying cities and a wilderness of ghost towns." [14]

The First Lady played an active part in promoting another environmental issue. Lady Bird Johnson traveled about 200,000 miles, crisscrossing the country many times, in a determined effort to get citizen support for improving the appearance of highways. She lobbied Congress to pass the Highway Beautification Act of 1965 (nicknamed the "Lady Bird Bill"), which called for the removal of billboards on sections of interstate and major highways that were not located in commercial or industrial zones.

The success of LBJ's many Great Society measures varied from program to program. Some, like federal aid to Appalachia, public housing, and the Job Corps, provided mainly short-term gains. Other measures, such as the extension of civil rights, Med-

177

icare and Medicaid, and environmental reforms, had more lasting benefits. However, the implementation of the programs set forth by the Great Society and the operation of its many agencies and departments vastly increased the national government's bureaucracy and cost the taxpayers much money.

In his conduct of foreign affairs, LBJ had to deal with troubled areas in various parts of the world. Early in his presidency, Johnson faced a serious problem in Panama. Rioting against United States citizens was set off by nationalists who wanted Panamanian sovereignty over the Canal Zone. Four U.S. soldiers and twenty-one Panamanians were killed in the fighting, and Panama broke off diplomatic relations with the United States. President Johnson faced this situation calmly and prudently. After he offered to review disputed issues fully and candidly, the rioting ended and Panama and the United States resumed diplomatic relations.

Another crisis erupted in April 1965, when a civil war broke out in the Dominican Republic between the U.S.-supported government forces and rebel troops backing former President Juan Bosch. President Johnson claimed that the insurgents were led by Communist conspirators and that Bosch intended to become a Communist dictator, like Fidel Castro in Cuba. Some Latin American experts disputed these claims, but LBJ, unwilling to risk the possible establishment of a second Communist regime in the Caribbean, sent in 20,000 soldiers. A few weeks later a truce was arranged pending a new presidential election, and United States troops were withdrawn when the Organization of American States provided a peace-keeping army to enforce the truce. As a result of this invasion the U.S. forces sustained 178 casualties and the ill will of Latin American countries that resented American interference in the internal affairs of a weaker neighbor.

The most serious problem that confronted the Johnson administration in international affairs was the role of the United States in the Vietnam War. To preserve its independence, the non-Communist government of South Vietnam was trying to repel invaders from Communist North Vietnam, who were aided by Communist forces (the Vietcong) inside South Vietnam. President Johnson felt committed to the containment policy first expounded by President Truman and later endorsed by Presidents Eisenhower and Kennedy: the Communists must be contained within their borders and not permitted to expand their territory at the expense of non-Communist countries. Furthermore, Johnson firmly believed that if South Vietnam fell to the Communists, it would be only a matter of time before other countries in Southeast Asia also would fall to Communist aggressors.

The Kennedy administration had provided both military advisers and financial aid to South Vietnam. When Johnson began his presidency, at first he adhered to the same policy of limited American involvement in the Vietnam War. Then, in August 1964, North Vietnamese gunboats allegedly fired on American ships in the Gulf of Tonkin. (Subsequent evidence revealed in a congressional inquiry cast serious doubts on the authenticity of the facts as originally reported.) The U.S. forces sank two of the enemy gunboats and bombed nearby bases in North Vietnam.

Congress reacted to this incident by passing the Gulf of Tonkin Resolution, which gave President Johnson power "to take all necessary measures to repel any armed attack against the forces of the United

States and to prevent further aggression."[15] This resolution was interpreted by LBJ as a blanket authorization for an all-out American commitment in the Vietnam War.

Attacks by the Vietcong on U.S. bases at Pleiku and Qui Nhon in February 1965 triggered heavy American bombing raids. The following month two battalions of marines, the first combat units from the United States, arrived in South Vietnam. By August 1965 the United States had armed forces consisting of 125,000 men on active duty in Vietnam; by 1966 this figure had risen to almost 400,000; it peaked in 1968, when 541,000 American military personnel were stationed in this Asian country.

Neither extensive bombing missions nor large-scale land assaults brought the Communists to their knees. As the war persisted and the number of American casualties mounted, a rising storm of criticism was unleashed at home. A growing number of senators and congressmen called for the withdrawal of all Americans from Vietnam. War protesters held angry rallies and demonstrations in many cities and towns. A number of frustrated young men burned their draft cards or left the country to avoid military service in a war they could not support.

President Johnson agonized over the tragic events in Vietnam and grieved when his Great Society program stalled because the war had greatly diminished his popularity with Congress and a large segment of the American public. He held countless staff meetings with military and diplomatic aides, pored over war maps, attempted various strategies, including temporary cessations of bombing raids, and proposed negotiated settlements with the Communists— all to no avail. Getting little sleep and preoccupied with trying to run a war that was essentially beyond his control, the president often appeared haggard,

180

weary, and listless. Yet he and his lieutenants, frantically hoping that someday the tide would turn, deceived the nation by exaggerating Communist losses and downgrading North Vietnam's will to continue the longest war in American history. And many times high officials in the Johnson administration falsely predicted an imminent victory for the combined forces of South Vietnam and the United States.

In January 1968 the North Vietnamese and the Viet Cong launched with unprecedented force an offensive against six South Vietnamese cities. It was militarily not successful for the Communists, but this giant offensive dealt a severe psychological blow to President Johnson because it convinced American public opinion that it was futile to maintain large-scale operations in Vietnam. A short time later the first 1968 presidential primary election was held in New Hampshire. Senator Eugene McCarthy, a Democratic "dove" who pledged to end American fighting in Vietnam, made a surprisingly strong showing, winning 42 percent of the votes.

Most political analysts had assumed that President Johnson would run for another term. But in a televised broadcast on March 31 he announced his decision not to seek reelection. In the same broadcast the president ordered the end of bombing north of the 21st parallel in North Vietnam and promised to spend his remaining months in the White House working to bring about peace in Vietnam.

Johnson was unable to end the war during his administration. When Richard M. Nixon became the next president in 1969, he instituted a program for the gradual removal of American troops from Vietnam. Finally, in January 1973, a cease-fire agreement was signed, calling for the withdrawal of the last American forces from battle-scarred Vietnam. Without American support, South Vietnam could not defend itself against renewed attacks from the north, and two years later, in April 1975, all of Vietnam became one Communist country. (More than 57,000 Americans lost their lives in the Vietnam War, and many more thousands were seriously injured.)

After Johnson left the White House he returned to his beloved LBJ Ranch on the banks of the Pedernales River. He helped manage his ranch operations, wrote his memoirs, and spent much time working to establish both a library to house his presidential papers and the Lyndon Baines Johnson School of Public Affairs at the University of Texas in Austin. On January 22, 1973, Johnson was stricken with a fatal heart attack. Ironically, he died in the same week that the Vietnam War came to an end.

Lyndon Johnson's five years in the presidency produced an exceptionally controversial administration. In 1964 and 1965 he pushed through Congress an incredible number of major bills designed to help bring about the Great Society. They met with varying degrees of success. His many-faceted program to improve the living standards of impoverished people drained Treasury funds and did not eradicate poverty. In fact, LBJ's so-called War on Poverty laid the groundwork for the widely shared opinion that huge government expenditures on social welfare measures do not necessarily produce desired results. In his State of the Union address in 1988, President Ronald Reagan asserted that "some years ago the federal government declared war on poverty, and poverty won." [16]

On the other hand, Johnson's administration left a legacy that included some notable achievements. The former Texas schoolteacher was the first president to persuade Congress to provide major educational benefits for American youth, from pre-

182

schoolers to college students. And he was the first chief executive to secure legislation that addressed the serious environmental problems caused by polluted air and water. Medicare was another landmark measure, offering inexpensive health care to the nation's elderly people. Among the most important accomplishments of the Johnson administration were the civil rights acts that barred discrimination in employment and public accommodations, provided minorities with equal voting rights, and guaranteed all citizens the same access to the sale and rental of housing. Minorities in the United States never had a better friend in the White House than LBJ.

Yet despite all that Johnson achieved on the home front, his record as president was fatally flawed by the dominant part he played in an unwinnable war fought in an area far from American shores. The president misled the public with optimistic predictions about the course of the war, relying more on his own earnest desires than on the actual battlefield reports. Lyndon Johnson gambled heavily on the first-rate military power of the United States being able to defeat the Communist armies of a small, underdeveloped Asian country—and he lost.

A once-popular president sadly watched the trust Americans had placed in him sink into the quicksand of Vietnam.

Chapter 10
Gerald R. Ford:
President by Appointment

Leslie King, Jr., was the name given at birth to the boy who became the thirty-eighth president of the United States. Born on July 14, 1913, in Omaha, Nebraska, he was the son of wool merchant Leslie King, Sr., and Dorothy Gardner King. When their child was two years old, Mrs. King divorced her husband and, taking young Leslie, went to live with her parents in Grand Rapids, Michigan. In 1916 Dorothy King married Gerald Rudolf Ford, who adopted her son and renamed him Gerald Rudolf Ford, Jr. (Later, the son changed the spelling of his middle name to Rudolph.)

Gerald Ford, Sr., a paint salesman in Grand Rapids, was a kind, considerate man and a devoted stepfather. Three more sons were born to him and his wife, and, although he was strict when they misbehaved, he treated all four boys equally and fairly. Gerald, Sr., impressed upon young Jerry the importance of hard work, honesty, and integrity. And by his many experiences in community and church af-

184

fairs, he showed how to be a good neighbor and share the concerns of others. Many years after Jerry had become an adult, he said that his stepfather had "the strongest influence on my life." [1]

There was always work to do around the Ford house, and Jerry, being the oldest child, had several chores. Outdoors, he mowed, raked, and watered the lawn, swept the sidewalks and porch, and, during the winter months, shoveled the snow from the driveway and sidewalks. Inside, he kept his room neat, helped with the dishes, and shoveled coal into the furnace and emptied the ashes. But there also was time for sports and enjoying the outdoors. The Ford boys and their dad swam and fished in nearby lakes, hiked in the woods, golfed, and played ball with the neighbors. Jerry also showed a keen interest in the Boy Scouts and worked up through the ranks of that organization until he achieved its highest honor—becoming an Eagle Scout.

In 1929 Gerald Ford, Sr., started his own paint factory, but that was the year of the stock market crash, and the ensuing depression nearly wiped out his business. The Ford family had to move to a less expensive home in a poorer section of Grand Rapids. As a high school student Jerry worked at odd jobs in the paint factory to earn some money. During his senior year he had a part-time job at a restaurant, where he waited on customers and washed dishes.

When Jerry had saved $75, he invested the money in a secondhand Model T Ford with a rumble seat. Returning from school one winter day, he parked his car in the driveway and noticed clouds of steam rising from its engine. Jerry hadn't bothered to pour antifreeze into the radiator, and he didn't realize that the motor had overheated in the cold weather. Thinking that it would be easier to start the car the next morning if the engine stayed warm overnight, he threw a blanket over it and went into the house for dinner. A short time later he heard the loud wail of fire engine sirens and, looking out a window, saw that his car was in flames. From then on, he had to take a long bus ride to and from school.

Jerry was an above-average student in high school. He excelled in history and government courses and did reasonably well in math, chemistry, and other sciences, but he had to struggle to earn a C in Latin.

His most notable achievements at Grand Rapids' South High School were in sports, not in the classroom. Tall, powerful, and very competitive, Jerry was a natural athlete. He was a good baseball and basketball player, but his best sport was football. Jerry wasn't a fleet-footed halfback or a pass-catching end; instead, he anchored the South High line at the position of center. For three years in a row he was named center on the All-City team. In 1930, Jerry's senior year, South High won the state championship and he was selected All-State center for the second consecutive season.

Following his high school graduation, Jerry entered the University of Michigan on a partial scholarship and majored in economics and political science. Because his family was still suffering financial setbacks and did not have funds to spare for Jerry's schooling, he took a job waiting on tables and occasionally earned a few extra dollars by donating blood at the university hospital. In his sophomore year Jerry joined the Delta Kappa Epsilon fraternity and paid for his room and board by washing dishes.

Jerry was a center on the Michigan freshman football team, and he won a trophy as the outstanding freshman player in spring practice. But after he moved up to the varsity team, Jerry did not have much playing time in his sophomore and junior years

186

because Michigan already had an All-American center, Chuck Bernard. Jerry had to wait until he was a senior and Bernard had graduated before he became the first-string center. He played so well then that at the end of the season he was named the most valuable member of the team. As an additional honor, he was chosen to play center in the 1935 College All-Stars game against the Chicago Bears.

Even though football and part-time jobs took much of his time, Jerry managed to graduate in the top quarter of his class. Both the Detroit Lions and Green Bay Packers offered him professional football contracts, but he turned them down because he was now interested in becoming a lawyer. However, he did not know how he would pay his way through law school. At that time, Yale University was looking for an assistant football coach. Young Mr. Ford from Michigan, who had never spent any time in the East, was offered the position if he would also agree to be the freshman boxing coach. Ford accepted the offer, hoping that it would be possible to begin his law studies at Yale while he was coaching there.

In his first year at Yale, Ford helped coach the football team to a season record of six victories and three losses. His second season was even better: Yale won the Ivy League championship with a record of seven wins and only one defeat. Among the players Ford helped coach that year were two future U.S. senators—Democrat William Proxmire and Republican Robert Taft, Jr.

Ford coached at Yale from 1935 through the 1940 season, but his plan to combine coaching with studying law was delayed because the law school frowned on enrolling a student who had to spend so much time on the football field. Three years passed before he was permitted to attend law classes. When

Ford finally was admitted to law school, in 1938, he worked hard at his studies. He was in the top third of his class when he received his law degree in 1941.

While he was at Yale, Ford began dating Phyllis Brown, an attractive New York fashion model. She talked him into taking a couple of modeling assignments. In March 1940, *Look* magazine ran a five-page feature article that included many pictures of the handsome, blond, 6-foot-tall football coach and his girlfriend. Ford's picture also appeared on the cover of *Cosmopolitan* magazine early in 1942. Jerry and Phyllis enjoyed a four-year courtship, but after he got his law degree, they went their separate ways because Phyllis wanted to stay in New York and Jerry was determined to go back to Grand Rapids.

With a college friend as his partner, Ford opened a law office in Grand Rapids in 1941. But that December their law practice was disrupted because the Japanese attacked Pearl Harbor and the United States was drawn into World War II. Ford was commissioned as a Navy ensign and sent to the Naval Academy at Annapolis, Maryland, for basic training. Because of his athletic record, after basic training he was assigned to work as a physical fitness instructor with the Navy's aviation cadets at the University of North Carolina. But Ford was eager for combat duty, and he wrote letters to Navy officers, requesting that he be transferred to a warship. After more than a year of waiting, he was assigned to the U.S.S. *Monterey*, a light aircraft carrier.

The *Monterey*—part of the Third Fleet, which saw heavy fighting in the South Pacific—often was attacked by Japanese planes. It managed to weather the air strikes, even when nearby American ships were sunk or badly damaged. The *Monterey*'s most hazardous encounter, however, was with a devastating typhoon that struck the Third Fleet in December 1944.

Eight hundred men were lost in that violent storm, which destroyed or damaged ten ships and nearly 200 planes. Ford later recalled his close brush with death when the typhoon lashed his ship:

> *As I stepped out on the flight deck, I lost my footing and slid across the deck like a toboggan. I put my feet out, and fortunately, my heels hit the little rim that surrounds the flight deck—I was heading straight for the ocean. I spun over onto my stomach and luckily dropped over the edge onto the catwalk just below. We lost five seamen or officers during that storm—sliding over the side and into the sea—so I guess I was one of the lucky ones.*[2]

After serving in the Navy almost four years and advancing to the rank of lieutenant commander, Ford resumed his law career in Grand Rapids. But he soon became vitally interested in politics. Before entering the armed forces, Ford had belonged to the isolationist wing of the Republican party; he then believed that the United States should not become involved in the affairs of other countries. His wartime experiences, however, caused him to change his mind about the role of the United States in the world. He emerged from World War II an ardent internationalist. Ford was convinced that the United States would need strong allies to resist the growing Communist threat and that the countries of Western Europe must receive much American help in order to rebuild their shattered economies and avert Communist takeovers.

In 1948 the congressional seat in Michigan's Fifth District was held by a Republican isolationist, Bartel J. Jonkman. He was an outspoken opponent of President Harry Truman's Marshall Plan, which was designed to provide money and materials that would aid the economic recovery of Western European nations. Internationalist Ford supported the Marshall Plan, and he decided to contest Jonkman for the Republican nomination in the congressional primary election. The odds were overwhelmingly against the young, virtually unknown lawyer's unseating a popular veteran congressman, but Ford waged a strenuous campaign day after day from early in the morning until late at night.

Meanwhile, Ford had been dating Elizabeth (Betty) Bloomer Warren, a pretty divorcée, who was a fashion coordinator at a Grand Rapids department store. Betty had studied dance under Martha Graham and worked several years as a dancer and model. Jerry proposed marriage to her in February 1948, but he told her, "We can't get married until next fall, and I can't tell you why."[3] She agreed to wait, and later he explained that he was going to run for a seat in Congress and their wedding would have to be delayed until after the Republican primary election.

Ford won a stunning upset victory over Jonkman, and in October he and Betty were married. But Jerry now was campaigning against his Democratic opponent in the general election, and he spent the morning of his wedding day meeting voters. He managed to change into a gray pin-striped suit for the ceremony but still was wearing the same dusty brown shoes he had worn campaigning earlier that day. The afternoon after their wedding Ford took his bride to a University of Michigan football game, and that night they attended a reception for New York Governor Thomas E. Dewey, the Republican who was running for the presidency against Democrat Harry Truman.

Michigan's Fifth District was solidly Republican, and Ford had little trouble defeating Democrat Fred

190

J. Barr in the general election. He and his wife then moved to Washington, D.C.; they remained in or near the nation's capital for the next twenty-eight years. During the 1950s the Fords had four children—sons Michael, John (Jack), and Steven, and daughter Susan.

As a young congressman, Ford listened carefully to debates, studied bills, learned political strategy, and worked hard to bring additional services to his Michigan constituents. He was exceedingly popular with the voters back home; they reelected him twelve times, each time with at least 60 percent of the vote. His leadership traits were recognized early in his political career; in 1949 the United States Junior Chamber of Commerce honored him as one of ten outstanding young Americans.

Congressman Ford considered himself a moderate in domestic affairs, a conservative in fiscal policy, and an internationalist in foreign affairs. He fought against expansion of the role of the national government in people's lives and had little faith in federal programs aimed at ending poverty and social inequality. Ford opposed federal aid to education, repeal of the Taft-Hartley Act, and emergency loans to farmers. He generally voted for civil rights bills but was criticized by minority leaders for attempting to weaken these bills through amendments. Ford favored most foreign aid measures, and he consistently voted for large defense appropriations. He criticized President Johnson for not pursuing the Vietnam War more aggressively, but he endorsed President Nixon's troop withdrawal and supported the 1973 peace treaty.

During his second term in office Ford was appointed to the important Appropriations Committee, which he served on for fourteen years. His diligent work on a subcommittee that studied military

191

spending made him one of Capitol Hill's foremost authorities on defense budgets.

The Michigan congressman first drew national attention in 1963 when he was elected chairman of the House Republican Conference, the third-ranking minority position in the House of Representatives. In that same year President Johnson apppointed Ford one of the two House members of the Warren Commission, which investigated the assassination of President Kennedy. Ford agreed with the Warren Commission's conclusion that Lee Harvey Oswald had acted alone in murdering the president. Later, he coauthored a book, *Portrait of the Assassin,* which gave the reasons why he did not believe that Kennedy's assassination stemmed from a conspiracy.

After the Democratic landslide in the congressional elections of 1964, Ford was convinced that the Republicans in the House needed new leadership. So he challenged the reelection of House Minority Leader Charles A. Halleck of Indiana. The election was close, but his colleagues gave Ford the top Republican position in the House by a vote of 73 to 67. The new minority leader was able to hold together the diverse groups within his party. Also, he was an able campaigner, averaging about 200 speeches a year in behalf of other Republican candidates. In the 1966 congressional elections he helped to win forty-seven more House seats for Republicans.

One of Ford's most controversial House activities was his attempt to instigate impeachment proceedings against Supreme Court Justice William O. Douglas, a liberal member of the high court. The Michigan congressman made five charges against Douglas, including the accusation that the Supreme Court justice had been a paid counsel to a foundation in violation of federal law. A special subcommittee of the House Judiciary Committee studied the charges and then voted that there were insufficient grounds for the impeachment of Douglas.

Minority Leader Ford's highest political ambition was to be speaker of the House, but this goal could not be reached as long as there were more Democrats than Republicans in the House. In every congressional election between 1954 and 1972, the Democrats retained control of the House and Ford glumly watched his hopes of becoming speaker grow dimmer and dimmer. He began thinking in 1973 about running just one more time for the House and, after completing that term, returning to Grand Rapids and his law practice.

Then suddenly something happened that dramatically altered Ford's career. In October 1973 Vice President Spiro T. Agnew, hounded by charges that he had accepted bribes and kickbacks while governor of Maryland, resigned from the second-highest office in the United States government. The vice presidency thus became vacant, for the eighth time in American history. When this had happened before, the position remained vacant until after the next election. But the Twenty-fifth Amendment, adopted in 1967, enables the president to appoint someone to fill the vice president's office, provided that person's nomination is confirmed by a majority vote of both houses of Congress.

President Richard M. Nixon named Gerald Ford the country's first unelected vice president. He knew that the former football player from Michigan had an absolutely clean record, was a political moderate known for his fairness and ability to compromise, and could work cooperatively with members of both houses of Congress. The Senate confirmed Ford's nomination by a 92–3 vote, the House by a 387–35 margin. Ford took the oath of office as the fortieth vice president on December 6, 1973.

The Republican party already was sagging under the weight of the Watergate scandal, which involved many members of the Nixon administration who were accused of breaking laws while helping the president win reelection in 1972. The new vice president traveled more than 100,000 miles and made about 500 appearances in a determined effort to rally his party. Ford expressed the belief that President Nixon, whom he had known as a friend and colleague for a quarter of a century, was not involved in the Watergate cover-up, but he urged the president to reveal all the evidence he had about this sordid affair.

Throughout the spring and early summer of 1974, public attention was riveted on the investigation that clearly showed Nixon had played a major role in the Watergate cover-up. The House of Representatives voted to impeach the beleaguered president. Rather than stand trial and in all likelihood be removed from office, Nixon resigned the presidency on August 9, 1974. That same day, at three minutes past noon, Gerald Ford was sworn in as the new president.

In a brief and moving address, President Ford told the nation:

> *I am acutely aware that you have not elected me as your President by your ballots. . . . In all my public and private acts as your President, I expect to follow my instincts of openness and candor with full confidence that honesty is always the best policy in the end. My fellow Americans, our long national nightmare is over. Our Constitution works; our great Republic is a government of laws and not of men.* [4]

The new president plunged into his job with energy and enthusiasm. He appointed former New York

194

Governor Nelson Rockefeller as vice president. While Rockefeller was too liberal to please right-wing Republicans, his nomination was confirmed by both houses of Congress. When Rockefeller took the oath of office on December 19, 1974, this was the first time in its history that the nation had both a president and a vice president not elected by the people.

Ford restored to the presidency the openness and candor that he had promised, which was much appreciated by both the public and the press. But early in his administration he made a controversial decision that caused his popularity to decline. The president was determined to take whatever steps he could to end the nation's long-standing preoccupation with the Watergate affair. So, one month after entering the White House, he granted a full pardon to former President Nixon for any or all offenses which he might have committed while he had been president. Ford explained his decision:

> *My conscience tells me clearly and certainly that I cannot prolong the bad dreams that continue to reopen a chapter that is closed. My conscience tells me that only I, as president, have the constitutional power to firmly shut and seal this book. My conscience tells me that it is my duty not merely to proclaim domestic tranquility but to use every means to insure it.*[5]

The response to the pardon from newspapers, members of Congress, and the general public was overwhelmingly negative. Many people criticized it as violating the principle of equal justice under the law, claiming that if President Nixon had been involved in crimes he should have been tried in court along with other Watergate defendants. Rumors circulated that a deal might have been made while Nixon was

still president—a deal in which Nixon agreed to resign in return for a promise that Ford would give
him a pardon.

There was such a storm of criticism over this issue that President Ford took the unprecedented step
of appearing before the House Judiciary Committee
to explain that there had been no deals connected
with the pardon. He assured the committee that the
pardon was prompted entirely by his strong desire
to end the agonizing Watergate ordeal. (Later, when
Ford commented on the pardon in his 1979 memoirs, he said that the humiliation of resigning the
presidency in disgrace was sufficient punishment, "the
equivalent to serving a jail term."[6])

Also in September 1974 President Ford con-
ceived a plan to give conditional amnesty to the
thousands of men who had evaded military service
during the Vietnam War. His program called for draft
evaders to receive clemency if they would swear an
oath of allegiance to the United States and perform
two years of public service. Deserters also were to be
granted amnesty, provided they swore allegiance and
served two years in the branch of the armed forces
from which they had escaped. When the program
ended in 1975, only about one-fifth of those eligible
had applied.

A combination of inflation, recession, and high
unemployment plagued the country when Ford assumed the presidency. At first he emphasized the fight
against inflation by proposing solutions that reflected
his philosophy of trying to have a balanced budget
and reduced expenditures, especially for social programs. He launched a highly publicized Whip Inflation Now (WIN) campaign, and thousands of WIN
buttons were distributed to those who agreed to hold
down prices and wages.

The recession deepened, however, and in early

196

1975 Ford reluctantly changed his approach to focus attention on relieving recession pressures rather than inflationary ones. The president supported legislation to reduce individual and corporate taxes by $16 billion in an attempt to stimulate the sluggish economy. He also signed into law bills that permitted the use of limited public funds for some new housing and other construction. But he was vehemently opposed to large public works programs and called for substantial reductions in government spending in order to keep the federal budget deficit as low as possible.

President Ford proposed few new spending programs of his own and resisted many of those initiated by Congress. In the course of his brief administration he vetoed about sixty bills, most of which called for additional federal expenditures. Even though Congress was controlled by the Democrats, it was able to override only about one-fifth of the president's vetoes.

The recession had eased by mid-1976, and industrial production was expanding. Inflation continued to hurt the consumer, but the rate of price increases dropped sharply. Unemployment declined, but in late 1976 it stood at 7.8 percent of the labor force, which was still high by historical standards.

Foreign problems also beset the Ford administration. In 1974 Congress denied the president's request for additional aid to the government of South Vietnam, which was tottering on the verge of extinction. When South Vietnam fell to the invading armies of Communist North Vietnam in April 1975, Ford ordered the immediate evacuation of remaining American personnel. At the same time hordes of frightened South Vietnamese fled their country by any means they could find. Many crowded into boats; a few even clung to the runners of helicopters. More than 100,000 Vietnamese refugees entered the United States and were resettled throughout the country.

Cambodia also fell to Communist insurgents, in April 1975. The following month Cambodian gunboats seized the *Mayaguez,* an American merchant ship, and took captive its thirty-nine crewmen. President Ford responded quickly, ordering air strikes and the landing of marines on the island where the crew was believed to be held. The operation was successful; the *Mayaguez* and its entire crew were rescued. However, forty-one American servicemen lost their lives in this mission.

Ford visited several countries during his administration. In November 1974 he became the first American president to go to Japan. He also visited China and the Soviet Union, where he met with Communist party leader Leonid Brezhnev. In Helsinki, Finland, Ford attended an important conference in which thirty-five nations, including the Soviet Union and most Iron Curtain countries, were represented. The leaders of these nations signed the Helsinki Accords, which promised that the borders of Eastern Europe would remain the same as they had been since World War II. The Helsinki Accords also included an agreement that every signatory nation would respect the basic human rights of all its citizens.

President Ford decided to run for a full four-year term in 1976. He first had to campaign in primary elections and state caucuses for the Republican nomination. His opponent was a popular, formidable candidate: charismatic Ronald Reagan, the former governor of California, who had powerful support in conservative regions. The race for the Republican nomination was the closest since 1920, when Warren G. Harding was selected on the tenth convention ballot. At the 1976 Republican convention, Ford won 1,187 delegate votes to Reagan's 1,070. Senator Robert Dole of Kansas was chosen as Ford's running mate.

Ford began the fall campaign as an underdog, and pollsters gave him little chance to defeat Democrat Jimmy Carter, the former governor of Georgia. A moralistic farmer from a small town, Carter appealed to many voters because he was not a wheeler-dealer "Washington insider" and he had no connection to the people who spawned Watergate. Ford was handicapped because many people still resented his pardoning of Nixon and also because he had never been elected to office in any area larger than Michigan's Fifth Congressional District.

The presidential candidates had three televised debates. Pollsters who measured public reaction believed that Ford had a slight edge in the first debate and Carter probably won the last two. The only serious blunder made by either candidate occurred in the second debate when Ford mistakenly said, "There is no Soviet domination of Eastern Europe."[7]

Ford trailed Carter by about 30 points in polls taken in September, but the gap narrowed steadily as the campaign progressed. By Election Day the race was too close to call. When the ballots were counted, Carter had a bare 50.1 percent of the popular vote and only 27 electoral votes more than the 270 needed to win. Ford had almost caught Carter at the finish line, but instead he became the first president in forty-four years to be turned out of office by the voters.

When he left the White House, Ford retired to his home in Rancho Mirage, California. He wrote his memoirs, served on the boards of several corporations, delivered many speeches, and enjoyed golf, swimming, and skiing as recreation.

In 1980 Ronald Reagan won the Republican presidential nomination, and he tried to convince Ford to be his running mate. This was a startling political development because there was no historical precedent for a former president's returning to Washington as a vice president. When the media speculated that Reagan and Ford, if elected, might be almost co-presidents, the proposal to run them on the same ticket was quickly dropped. George Bush then was selected as the party's vice presidential nominee.

Always loyal to the Republican cause, Ford campaigned vigorously for the Reagan-Bush ticket, covering 60,000 miles and speaking in thirty states. No other former Republican president had ever traveled so far or made so many public appearances in behalf of other candidates.

The presidency was at its lowest ebb when Gerald Ford stepped into the office. The disastrous Vietnam War followed quickly by the devastating Watergate scandal had caused countless Americans to lose faith in the person who occupied the highest position in the national government. Ford brought back honesty and integrity to the office that Lyndon Johnson had misused and Richard Nixon had abused. He worked tirelessly to bind up the deep wounds that had torn the nation apart. President Jimmy Carter paid tribute to this notable achievement in the first words of his inaugural address. Turning from the podium and looking at Ford, he declared, "For myself and for our nation, I want to thank my predecessor for all he has done to heal our land."[8]

The Ford administration did not leave a long record of major domestic accomplishments. This was partly because the Democrats ruled Congress and Ford felt it was necessary to veto repeated congressional requests for increased federal spending. Also, it was partly because Ford served less than two and one-half years in the White House during a period following great turbulence, and, unlike most new presidents, he had neither the time nor the supportive political atmosphere needed to develop many long-range programs. Except for Warren G. Harding, Gerald Ford had the shortest term of any president in the twentieth century.

Epilogue

There is no simple formula for determining whether the accidental presidents were efficient and effective chief executives. In a 1962 poll conducted by Arthur M. Schlesinger, Sr., seventy-five historians were asked to rank the presidents. They ranked Theodore Roosevelt and Harry Truman in the "near-great" category, Chester Alan Arthur and Andrew Johnson as "average" presidents, and John Tyler, Millard Fillmore, and Calvin Coolidge as "below-average."[1] (Lyndon Johnson and Gerald Ford served as presidents after the poll was conducted.)

If the success of accidental presidents should be based on their popularity with voters, then the criterion might be whether they were elected to a full four-year term. Four of them—Theodore Roosevelt, Coolidge, Truman, and Lyndon Johnson—won presidential terms of their own. The five others—Tyler, Fillmore, Andrew Johnson, Arthur, and Ford—were not returned to the White House after completing the terms of prior presidents whom they succeeded in office.

Popular appeal, however, is not necessarily a fair yardstick to use in assessing the permanent effects of a president's administration. Coolidge and Lyndon Johnson both won landslide victories at the polls, but the long-range view of history casts serious doubts on their use of presidential power. Coolidge failed to exert enough power to come to grips with many of the nation's problems; Johnson overextended his power, trying to bring about vast social and economic changes at home while masterminding the only war that the United States ever lost.

On the other hand, some accidental presidents were denied a four-year term mainly because they had taken stands on issues that were unpopular in their time. Fillmore's approval of the Fugitive Slave Act cost him the support of the North, the region with which he was most closely identified. Andrew Johnson endured a humiliating impeachment trial primarily because he had tried to enforce moderate Reconstruction policies that were strongly resisted by Congress. Ford was an honest president who had the misfortune of pardoning a dishonest president and leading a party that the public wanted to punish for the sordid Watergate affair. Arthur also was an honest president, but he could never quite make the voters forget that he once had been a spoilsman and machine politician. And poor Tyler suffered through a tormented administration because he could not support the major policies of the Whig party that had run him for vice president in order to win southern votes.

Every accidental president has been expected, in varying degrees, to follow a path laid down by another man, one who had been elected to hold this

204

office. The task of filling someone else's shoes is seldom an easy one. Much is asked of the understudy who suddenly is called upon to perform the leading role in a play, or the substitute quarterback who, at a moment's notice, is thrust into the position of directing his team's strategy.

Some accidental presidents have ridden the tiger and fulfilled their duties better than others. All of them, however, have adhered to this pledge made by Gerald Ford when he assumed the highest office in the land: "I have not sought this enormous responsibility, but I will not shirk it."[2]

Source Notes

Prologue

1. James David Barber, *The Presidential Character* (Englewood Cliffs, N.J.: Prentice-Hall, 1972), p. 271.

Chapter 1

1. Theodore Roosevelt, "The Three Vice-Presidential Candidates," *Review of Reviews,* September 1896, p. 292.
2. Roy Hoopes, *The Changing Vice-Presidency* (New York: Crowell, 1981), p. 1.
3. Arthur M. Schlesinger, Jr., *The Cycles of American History* (Boston: Houghton Mifflin, 1986), p. 337.
4. Donald Young, *American Roulette: The History and Dilemma of the Vice Presidency* (New York: Holt, Rinehart and Winston, 1972), p. 5.
5. Hoopes, p. 2.
6. Jack W. Germond and Jules Witcover, *Whose*

Broad Stripes and Bright Stars: The Trivial Pursuit of the Presidency 1988 (New York: Warner, 1989), p. 442.

7. Schlesinger, p. 342.
8. Walter F. Mondale, "How a Vice President Should Handle His Leader," *Akron Beacon Journal,* March 15, 1981, p. G-5.
9. Germond and Witcover, p. 370.

Chapter 2

1. Robert Seager, II, *And Tyler Too* (New York: McGraw-Hill, 1963), p. 52.
2. Eugene H. Roseboom and Alfred E. Eckes, Jr., *A History of Presidential Elections,* 4th ed. (New York: Macmillan, 1979), p. 54.
3. Donald Young, *American Roulette: The History and Dilemma of the Vice Presidency* (New York: Holt, Rinehart and Winston, 1972), p. 42.
4. Seager, p. 149.
5. Young, p. 47.
6. Paul F. Boller, Jr., *Presidential Anecdotes* (New York: Oxford University Press, 1981), p. 96.
7. Sid Frank and Arden Davis Melick, *The Presidents: Tidbits and Trivia* (Maplewood, N.J.: Hammond, 1982), p. 100.
8. Seager, p. 207.

Chapter 3

1. Paul F. Boller, Jr., *Presidential Campaigns* (New York: Oxford University Press, 1984), p. 85.
2. *The American Heritage Pictorial History of the Presidents of the United States* (New York: American Heritage, 1968), vol. 1, p. 329.
3. John D. Feerick, *From Falling Hands: The Story of Presidential Succession* (New York: Fordham University Press, 1965), p. 102.

4. Jane McConnell and Burt McConnell, *Our First Ladies: Martha Washington to Pat Ryan Nixon* (New York: Crowell, 1969), pp. 144–145.
5. Sid Frank and Arden Davis Melick, *The Presidents: Tidbits and Trivia* (Maplewood, N.J.: Hammond, 1982), p. 101.
6. Sol Barzman, *Madmen and Geniuses: The Vice-Presidents of the United States* (Chicago: Follett, 1974), p. 89.

Chapter 4

1. *The American Heritage Pictorial History of the Presidents of the United States* (New York: American Heritage, 1968), vol. 1, p. 430.
2. Ibid., p. 431.
3. Michael V. DiSalle and Lawrence G. Blochman, *Second Choice* (New York: Hawthorn Books, 1966), p. 73.
4. Gene Smith, *High Crimes and Misdemeanors: The Impeachment and Trial of Andrew Johnson* (New York: Morrow, 1977) p. 66.
5. Ibid.
6. Lloyd Paul Stryker, *Andrew Johnson: A Study in Courage* (New York: Macmillan, 1929), p. 218.
7. Edmund Lindop, *By a Single Vote! One-Vote Decisions That Changed American History* (Harrisburg, Pa.: Stackpole Books, 1987), p. 54.

Chapter 5

1. Thomas C. Reeves, *Gentleman Boss: The Life of Chester Alan Arthur* (New York: Knopf, 1975), p. 62.
2. Edmund Lindop, *All about Republicans* (Hillside, N.J.: Enslow, 1985), p. 19.
3. Reeves, p. 180.
4. Ibid., p. 183.

5. "The Week," *The Nation,* June 17, 1880, p. 445.
6. Justus D. Doenecke, *The Presidencies of James A. Garfield and Chester Alan Arthur* (Lawrence, Kans.: Regents Press of Kansas, 1981), p. 27.
7. Ibid., p. 39.
8. Reeves, p. 237.
9. Ibid., p. 241.

Chapter 6

1. Edmund Lindop and Joseph Jares, *White House Sportsman* (Boston: Houghton Mifflin, 1964), p. 45.
2. William A. DeGregorio, *The Complete Book of U.S. Presidents* (New York: Dembner Books, 1984), p. 376.
3. Edmund Morris, *The Rise of Theodore Roosevelt* (New York: Coward, McCann & Geoghegan, 1979), p. 73.
4. Lindop and Jares, pp. 46–47.
5. Noel Busch, *T.R.: The Story of Theodore Roosevelt and His Influence on Our Times* (New York: Reynal, 1963), p. 37.
6. Fletcher Pratt, *The Navy: A History* (Garden City, N.Y.: Garden City Publishing, 1941), p. 360.
7. Paul F. Boller, Jr., *Presidential Campaigns* (New York: Oxford University Press, 1984), p. 180.
8. DeGregorio, pp. 385–386.
9. Lindop and Jares, p. 49.
10. Boller, p. 193.
11. Nicholas Roosevelt, *Theodore Roosevelt: The Man as I Knew Him* (New York: Dodd, Mead, 1967), p. 71.
12. Busch, p. 1.
13. *The American Heritage Pictorial History of the Presidents of the United States* (New York: American Heritage, 1968), vol. 2, p. 656.

Chapter 7

1. Claude M. Fuess, *Calvin Coolidge: The Man from Vermont* (Hamden, Conn.: Archon Books, 1965), p. 25.
2. Donald R. McCoy, *Calvin Coolidge: The Quiet President* (New York: Macmillan, 1967), p. 49.
3. Michael DiSalle and Lawrence G. Blochman, *Second Choice* (New York: Hawthorn Books, 1966), p. 132.
4. Paul F. Boller, Jr., *Presidential Campaigns* (New York: Oxford University Press, 1984), p. 213.
5. McCoy, p. 121.
6. *National Party Conventions, 1831–1976* (Washington, D.C.: Congressional Quarterly Inc., 1979), p. 52.
7. McCoy, p. 148.
8. Boller, p. 218.
9. McCoy, p. 193.
10. Fuess, p. 300.
11. *Cleveland Plain Dealer,* May 29, 1981, p. 8-D.

Chapter 8

1. Cabell Phillips, *The Truman Presidency: The History of a Triumphant Succession* (New York: Macmillan, 1966), p. 11.
2. Frank McNaughton and Walter Hehmeyer, *This Man Truman* (New York: McGraw-Hill, 1945), p. 69.
3. Phillips, p. 30.
4. Ibid., p. 44.
5. Paul F. Boller, Jr., *Presidential Campaigns* (New York: Oxford University Press, 1984), pp. 260–261.
6. Phillips, p. 6.
7. *Los Angeles Times,* August 29, 1989, part 1, p. 9.

Chapter 9

1. Dudley Lynch, *The President from Texas: Lyndon Baines Johnson* (New York: Crowell, 1975), p. 3.
2. Alfred Steinberg, *Sam Johnson's Boy: A Close-up of the President from Texas* (New York: Macmillan, 1968), p. 30.
3. Merle Miller, *Lyndon: An Oral Biography* (New York: Putnam, 1980), pp. 26–27.
4. Paul K. Conkin, *Big Daddy from the Pedernales: Lyndon Baines Johnson* (Boston: Twayne, 1986), p. 118.
5. Lynch, p. 74.
6. Conkin, p. 177.
7. William A. DeGregorio, *The Complete Book of U.S. Presidents* (New York: Dembner Books, 1984), p. 574.
8. Stanley Meisler, "Can L.B.J.'s Great Society Ever Exist?" *Los Angeles Times*, July 14, 1989, part I, p. 20.
9. *National Party Conventions, 1831–1976* (Washington, D.C.: Congressional Quarterly Inc., 1979), p. 103.
10. Paul F. Boller, Jr., *Presidential Campaigns* (New York: Oxford University Press, 1984), p. 311.
11. Meisler, p. 20.
12. Lynch, p. 128.
13. Ibid.
14. Albert M. Schlesinger, Jr., *The Almanac of American History* (New York: Putnam, 1983), p. 578.
15. Ibid., pp. 568–569.
16. Meisler, p. 20.

Chapter 10

1. Jerald F. terHorst, *Gerald Ford and the Future of the Presidency* (New York: The Third Press, 1974), p. 34.

2. Ibid., p. 48.
3. Sallie Randolph, *Gerald R. Ford, President* (New York: Walker, 1987), p. 54.
4. terHorst, p. 188.
5. Randolph, p. 79.
6. Gerald R. Ford, *A Time to Heal* (New York: Harper & Row, 1979), p. 168.
7. Edmund Lindop, *All about Republicans* (Hillside, N.J.: Enslow, 1985), p. 79.
8. Randolph, p. 104.

Epilogue

1. William A. DeGregorio, *The Complete Book of U.S. Presidents* (New York: Dembner Books, 1984), p. x.
2. Sallie Randolph, *Gerald R. Ford, President* (New York: Walker, 1987), p. 75.

For Further Reading

Boller, Paul F., Jr. *Presidential Anecdotes.* New York: Oxford University Press, 1981.

————. *Presidential Campaigns.* New York: Oxford University Press, 1984.

Busch, Noel. *T.R.: The Story of Theodore Roosevelt and His Influence on Our Times.* New York: Reynal, 1963.

Conkin, Paul K. *Big Daddy from the Pedernales: Lyndon Baines Johnson.* Boston: Twayne, 1986.

DeGregorio, William A. *The Complete Book of U.S. Presidents.* New York: Dembner Books, 1984.

DiSalle, Michael V., and Lawrence G. Blochman. *Second Choice.* New York: Hawthorn Books, 1966.

Doenecke, Justus D. *The Presidencies of James A. Garfield and Chester Alan Arthur.* Lawrence, Kans.: Regents Press of Kansas, 1981.

Feerick, John D. *From Falling Hands: The Story of Presidential Succession.* New York: Fordham University Press, 1965.

Frank, Sid, and Arden Davis Melick. *The Presidents: Tidbits and Trivia.* Maplewood, N.J.: Hammond, 1982.

Fuess, Claude M. *Calvin Coolidge: The Man from Vermont.* Hamden, Conn.: Archon Books, 1965.

Hoopes, Roy. *The Changing Vice-Presidency.* New York: Crowell, 1981.

Light, Paul C. *Vice-Presidential Power: Advice and Influence in the White House.* Baltimore: Johns Hopkins University Press, 1984.

Lillegard, Dee. *John Tyler, Tenth President of the United States.* Chicago: Childrens Press, 1987.

Lindop, Edmund. *All about Republicans.* Hillside, N.J.: Enslow, 1985.

Lindop, Edmund, and Joy Crane Thornton. *All about Democrats.* Hillside, N.J.: Enslow, 1985.

Lynch, Dudley. *The President from Texas: Lyndon Baines Johnson.* New York: Crowell, 1975.

McCoy, Donald R. *Calvin Coolidge: The Quiet President.* New York: Macmillan, 1967.

Miller, Merle. *Lyndon: An Oral Biography.* New York: Putnam, 1980.

Miller, Richard Lawrence. *Truman: The Rise to Power.* New York: McGraw-Hill, 1986.

Morris, Edmund. *The Rise of Theodore Roosevelt.* New York: Coward, McCann and Geoghegan, 1979.

Osborne, John. *White House Watch: The Ford Years.* Washington, D.C.: New Republic Books, 1977.

Phillips, Cabell. *The Truman Presidency: The History of a Triumphant Succession.* New York: Macmillan, 1966.

Randolph, Sallie G. *Gerald R. Ford, President.* New York: Walker, 1987.

Rayback, Robert J. *Millard Fillmore: Biography of a President.* East Aurora, N.Y.: Henry Stewart, 1959.

Reeves, Thomas C. *The Life of Chester Alan Arthur.* New York: Knopf, 1975.

Seager, Robert, II. *And Tyler Too.* New York: McGraw-Hill, 1963.

Sindler, Allan P. *Unchosen Presidents: The Vice-President and Other Frustrations of Presidential Succession.* Berkeley: University of California Press, 1976.

216

Smith, Gene. *High Crimes and Misdemeanors: The Impreachment and Trial of Andrew Johnson.* New York: Morrow, 1977.

Stampp, Kenneth M. *The Era of Reconstruction, 1865–1877.* New York: Knopf, 1965.

terHorst, Jerald F. *Gerald Ford and the Future of the Presidency.* New York: The Third Press, 1974.

Trefousse, Hans L. *Andrew Johnson: A Biography.* New York: Norton, 1989.

Young, Donald. *American Roulette: The History and Dilemma of the Vice Presidency.* New York: Holt, Rinehart and Winston, 1972.

Index

218